REBEL SUCCESS FOR LEADERS

LEAD, GROW AND SELL FEARLESSLY

CHARLOTTE ALLEN
THE REBEL LEADER

WHAT PEOPLE ARE SAYING

"Charlotte Allen is the visionary authority on leadership success."

—SARAH VICTORY, INTERNATIONAL AWARD-WINNING
SPEAKER AND AUTHOR OF TWO BEST SELLERS
THEVICTORYCOMPANY.COM

"*Rebel Success for Leaders* highlights areas where you can identify real-life next steps to get the results you want and the results you need—quickly and effectively!"

—WENDY K. BENSON, MBA, OTR/L AND ELIZABETH A. MYERS, RN,
CO-AUTHORS, *THE CONFIDENT PATIENT*, 2X2 HEALTH:
PRIVATE HEALTH CONCIERGE, HTTP://WWW.2X2HEALTH.COM/

"To all serial 'disruptive innovators,' put this book on the top of your reading list!"

—LESLIE MACLIN, PRINCIPAL, ISTHMUS INNOVATION

"Charlotte's book outlines how you can spread this mindset to your team and positively impact your work environment."

—FRANNY GILMAN, DIRECTOR OF R&D AT TERRAMAX

"Rebel Success has useful insights that will help you level up your leadership! Anyone looking to bring out their inner rebel and lean into leadership will benefit from the strategies in this book."

—MARK STEEL, KEYNOTE SPEAKER AND SALES CONSULTANT, FOUNDER OF PEAK POTENTIAL, AND AUTHOR OF *INVINCIBLE SUCCESS: SELL WITH CONFIDENCE, LEAD WITH PURPOSE, AND SPEAK WITH IMPACT*

"Finally, a simple and easy-to-understand guide on leadership development."

—DR. KIMBERLY SCHEHRER, TEEN BREAKTHROUGH EXPERT, FOUNDER OF ACADEMY FOR INDEPENDENCE, AND PODCAST HOST OF "RAISING UNSTOPPABLE TEENS" ON VOICE AMERICA AND ITUNES

"*Rebel Success for Leaders* is a very timely book with a wonderful blend of inspiring stories and actionable steps to take and create rebel leadership and culture within yourself or your organizations."

—ROGER ZELLNER, PRESIDENT AND OWNER, ROGUE ZEBRA CONSULTING, WWW.ROGUEZEBRA.COM

"Charlotte shares wonderful personal experiences teaching professionals how to lead, grow, and become fearless in the pursuit of success."

—DR. IVAN SALABERRIOS, CEO, AIM TECHNICAL CONSULTANTS, INC., HTTPS://AIMTECHNICAL.COM

"If you want to accelerate from slow evolution to the super expressway of rapid innovation, Charlotte Allen's book is the key. You must read this book!"

—Dr. Vince Racioppo, international speaker, author, and consultant; President of the Center for Expert Performance, Inc.

"I found this book to be smart, insightful, and disruptive versus the everyday leadership book!"

—Kristin Crockett, CEO, Courageous Destiny, WWW.COURAGEOUSDESTINY.COM

"*Rebel Success* is the inescapable battle cry for you to step into your own Rebel Success."

—Suzanne K Nance, world record holder, speaker, and author HTTPS://WWW.LEADFROMTHETOP.COM/

RHG | MEDIA PRODUCTIONS™

Rebel Success for Leaders:

How to Lead, Grow and Sell Fearlessly

Copyright © 2020 by Charlotte Allen

RHG Media Productions

25495 Southwick Drive #103

Hayward, CA 94544.

ISBN 978-1735483207 paperback

ISBN 978-1735483214 hardcover

Visit us on line at www.YourPurposeDrivenPractice.com

Printed in the United States of America.

CONTENTS

Foreword 9

Acknowledgments 13

Part One - The Future Belongs to Rebels 15

    Chapter One - Rebel Beginnings 17

    Chapter Two - Rebel Unwrapped 29

    Chapter Three - Go for Impact 31

    Chapter Four - Famous Rebels 35

    Chapter Five - Power of the Rebel 37

    Chapter Six - Translating the Unconventional 41

Part Two - Rebel Success Secrets 43

    Chapter Seven - The Profit Factor 45

    Chapter Eight - Find and Unleash Your Rebel Talent 51

    Chapter Nine - Go Off-Road for Best Results 65

    Chapter Ten - Believe in Your Rebels 79

    Chapter Eleven - Discover Your Best Rebel 83

    Chapter Twelve - Up Your Rebel Magnetism 87

Chapter Thirteen - How to Have Limitless Energy 93

Chapter Fourteen - Selling and Influencing 101

Chapter Fifteen - Nothing but Upside 113

Part Three - Unleash the Revolution of Innovation 119

Chapter Sixteen - Unstoppable 121

Chapter Seventeen - Align, Activate, Cultivate 125

Chapter Eighteen - The Sustained Advantage 135

Chapter Nineteen - Start the Revolution 141

Chapter Twenty - Own the Gap 147

Chapter Twenty-One - Evolve Your Rebel Talent 149

Chapter Twenty-Two - Invest in Your Rebel Talent 153

Chapter Twenty-Three - Live It Now! 157

Rebel Success for Leaders 161

Bonus - Exclusive Invitation 163

Appendix - Level Up Activities 165

About the Author 175

Reviews 177

FOREWORD

Dr. Cheryl A. Lentz

"I've learned that people will forget what you said, people will forget what you did, but people will never forget how you made them feel."
—*Maya Angelou*

Leadership is the ability to connect to the human spirit. This idea of connection encapsulates the nature of this book. How do you lead yourself and connect with others to make a difference? Leadership is not a position we have or a title we hold; it is an action we take. Leadership is who we are at our very core.

At the most basic level, leadership has two choices—tasks or people. Do we focus on *what* we do—the task orientation—or do we focus on the people, the relationship orientation? Take care of your people, and they will take care of you. Simple. Not always easy.

The question is not always *what* we do but *how* we do it. One size does not fit all.

"If all we have is a hammer, coincidentally,
everything looks like a nail."
—Abraham Maslow

We cannot control how others show up in the world; we can only control how we do. The secret? As we show up differently, so will our followers as they follow our lead. Leadership is about influence, about offering an example *worthy of being followed.*

The focus of this book is on a unique aspect of leadership—the innovator, the forward thinker, leading from the front, the non-conformist—what this book calls **the Rebel leader.**

I more than understand what it means to be a Rebel as I have spent a career seemingly always being a square peg in the proverbial round hole, always challenging the status quo to the chagrin of my bosses and colleagues. I am usually the one on the fringes of being in the in-group. Even among leaders, we often march to the beat of a different drummer. Conformity isn't our thing. Fitting in isn't our thing (even though I love it when it happens!). It is simply our nature to question everything we see, not out of a desire to be difficult, but from a desire to seek solutions.

While leadership and business fundamentals are fundamentals for a reason, those who push the boundaries ultimately lead the leaders. And this *how* is as unique as the points of a snowflake, no two ever being exactly alike.

Many might ask *why*. In the world of refractive thinking, we often ask *why not, what if,* and *what's next.* We don't live in a world of what was, but what could be, and we will lead in this direction.

Few leaders ever wish to be the same as everyone else, as this Rebel leader referred to in this book. The rebel is one who challenges the status quo, not who stands behind it. For many managers, if it ain't broke, don't fix it. For the Rebel leader, if it ain't broke, perhaps it ought to be. Tell someone it can't be done; they might just find a way to prove you wrong, and this is what motivates the Rebel leader. They won't get mad, but they will get motivated. Results speak for themselves. It is only impossible until someone does it.

Unique, unconventional, seeing what is already there with new eyes—are all parts of those who see the world through a much different lens. Thank goodness for these unique leaders who have shaped the world we live in. Malcolm Gladwell, in his book *The Outliers*, suggested that we might learn more from the one unique outlier running as fast as possible than the 10,000 people going in the opposite direction. What does this one person know or see that the others missed? Sometimes the majority is just that—the majority—and they have been known to be wrong.

One does not have to follow the crowd. Innovators, refractive thinkers, and Rebels are those who ask different questions, envision what others cannot or will not see, seeing a vastly different path forward or simply building a new one. Learning to lead from this authentic uniqueness often takes courage, conviction, a strong personality, confidence, and a willingness to perhaps get it wrong and fail a few times until they get it right, but always rising to the challenge to get up and try again and again, and again—however long it takes. Failure is their ally, and failure has no alibi. No excuses here. No place to hide. These types of leaders are relentless, resilient, determined, and persistent. They will find a way. Just watch them.

The strength of this book lies in its ability to offer suggested solutions to see the world through the eyes of a rebel leader. Do not be afraid to shake things up, to go a different direction, to intentionally be a contrarian, to question everything in the quest to find a different and successful path forward.

Lead, follow, or get out of the way.

Learn to be bold. Learn to take action. Learn there are strength and power in one. Learn to be a Rebel.

See you around the quad!

Dr. Cheryl

The Academic Entrepreneur

Website: www.DrCherylLentz.com

Email: drcheryllentz@gmail.com

ACKNOWLEDGMENTS

To my husband Scott: for always believing in me.

To my son Ryan: for always challenging me to be fearless.

To my parents: for the support to explore my vision and the determination to stick with it.

To all the many mentors I've had and the ones yet to come: because without mentors, we don't grow to our full potential.

PART ONE

THE FUTURE BELONGS TO REBELS

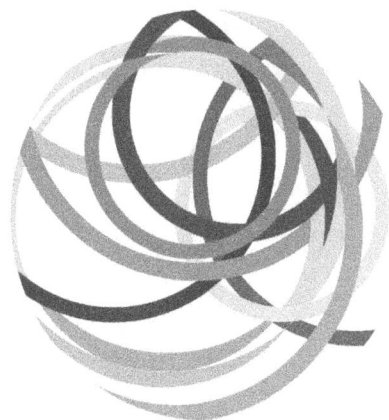

PART ONE

THE FUTURE BELONGS TO REBELS

CHAPTER ONE

REBEL BEGINNINGS

It was 5:00 a.m. in late July, and I had just been called awake even though it was summer vacation. Life on a farm always started early and finished late. The sun wasn't up yet, and I was allowed about ten minutes to dress and eat. I pulled on the dirty farm clothes that were in a pile—outside clothes that you wore for many days in a row before washing. These had three days of dirt, mud, and sweat clinging to them. Someone else would have said they smelled, but when you wore them every day, you didn't really notice. I grabbed a piece of yesterday's cornbread with jam and ate that with a glass of real milk, or what other people would call "whole milk." After that, I trudged up to the garden—really a small field. With no air conditioning in the house in the summer, you never really slept well for months. When you went outside, the humidity hit you in the face and was thick enough to cut with a knife. Even though it would be over ninety degrees that day, you wore long pants and long sleeves. At 5:00 a.m., it could be called cool. Shoes could be found out on the porch and were filled with yesterday's dirt.

The walk was in the dark and mostly quiet. When reaching the garden, you were assigned your row. You either planted all kinds of vegetables, used a hoe to till up the dirt mostly for potatoes, or weeded a whole lot of green beans and lima beans. You learned methods and processes for how to do it well, or you did it again. You also learned how to do it efficiently, so you finished faster before it got too hot. Up one side of the row and down the other as sweat began to form, and the day got hotter. Thirst took over, and you may be allowed a break, but that was closely monitored for lost productivity. There was a break for lunch and an attempt to nap in the hottest part of the day only because there wasn't much else to do. As evening approached, more work, but this time there were mosquitoes to contend with. They buzzed around your sweat, and you itched into mindless oblivion. Returning to the house always meant a change to inside clothes. The next day repeated the prior.

The simple life. Outdoors, nature, time to play and run around, connected to the land on the farm. Livestock and growing your own produce to sustain the family. This may sound like an ideal life, but it was not going to be my future life.

No one moved away and struck out on their own. If you weren't successful, that was just the way it was, but you didn't relocate. If you were a girl, your only future was in marriage and maybe becoming a teacher—my entire being itched for more than rural farming Maryland had to offer. I rebelled against the expected norm. No one I knew had left the community, but no matter what, I wasn't staying—no future for me on the farm. Work and school were the paths to more, better, security, and happiness.

I dedicated myself to my first job, working hard, causing no trouble, and being reliable. I learned a valuable lesson when I stood up for what I believed to be right. One of the other stores had been robbed late at night, and I didn't want to work late at night by myself. So, they fired me! Through high school, I worked many jobs to make money for college. I dressed up in a Pink Panther costume in July on the weekends and waved at people to advertise insulation for a new housing development. I seated tired travelers and cleaned grease traps at an interstate rest area. The place was run by two old military sergeants, and it was the only stop for fifty miles. The best perk of that job was eating my two complimentary crab cakes per shift—legitimate crab cakes, very yummy!

College came, and I left home for a city school that was in every way the exact opposite of how I had grown up. Everyone wore black; there were a lot of commuters, an X-rated theater three blocks away. It was overwhelming, lonely, and super different. I hunkered down to the grades and classes and learned to meet new and different people. I was nominated for a special program for pre-med students: on-the-job-training for respiratory therapy. They were recruiting bachelor of science students into that field. It offered me exposure to the medical field, where I wanted to be.

It was a great job during college, and it paid well—perfect for the type-A, twenty-something who thought it was pretty cool to work forty hours in three days and then have the rest of the week off. I finished my bachelor's and completed the respiratory therapy credentials in six weeks in an accelerated program versus two years, providing much-needed money for medical school.

For the first time, I had a job that many people consider a career, with good pay, benefits, opportunity. It was better than a paid internship, working in my field of interest, though not the role I ultimately desired. I learned a lot about the science of respiratory disease, what was important, how to work with the staff, nurses, doctors, and patients. More importantly, I learned how the "medical system" worked. I worked hard to be knowledgeable, professional, and efficient, and I took great care to ensure patients were looked after and were breathing as comfortably as possible. I had a great reputation.

The comfort bubble burst with just one event. I was summoned to provide a deposition for a court case where a patient's outcome after surgery was not what anyone expected. My mind was swirling, and at the same time, my stress level was climbing, going through every detail of what happened in my mind, and sure I did the right thing correctly. Stories were everywhere of people, not just losing their jobs but also their career potential over lawsuits. I didn't sleep for three days before the deposition and threw up in the bathroom of the law office just before going in. I spent three hours in the office getting grilled with all sorts of questions. I left completely disoriented and exhausted. The questions of what this means for my future and how it would play out just kept coming. When I finish medical school and become a doctor, how often would I have this experience? Would patients and families be more likely to bring lawsuits?

As I'm walking into a patient's room, I'm wondering if maybe I needed to rethink my career choice. The room was small and functional, with no decorations or comfort touches with two hospital beds, and only one was occupied. The big TV was hanging from the wall across from both beds, meaning they had to agree on what was watched. The bathroom had handicapped rails, a sink, and a toilet. The window was small with blinds and faced a tree in the courtyard. The radiator/air conditioner was under the window and hummed or rattled when it ran. The room was hot, as most patients were always cold.

A woman was in the center of her bed, propped up only slightly. She was under what had to be six hospital blankets that also reached up to her ears. The other arm was less covered only because it had the IV. One small lap blanket was on her bed and embroidered with a floral print. She was small, less than five feet tall, thin, and frail. She left you with the impression that she would fall over if you talked too loudly.

She was a regular lung patient, which meant that standing or sitting, her body was always hunched over, and she breathed with her body. It seemed like her lungs weren't enough to draw breath. For her, breathing wasn't effortless, and she always needed oxygen. Every breath was taken through pursed or puckered lips, never a fully open mouth. She was elderly, a darker-skinned black woman, hair that had once been black but was now grayed and cut very close. Her hands and arms are the kind that you can not only see the veins but can also easily pick out some of the smaller bones.

Her face was lined deeply, especially the line between her eyebrows. Her life was etched on her face, the good and mostly the difficulties. Her eyes were amazing, though. They were the kind of eyes that were wise and filled with love and knowing. They bore deep inside you when she looked at you, making you feel good but also slightly uncomfortable. She had the gift of always being present, meaning she was never anywhere but right there with you. When she reached out to touch your hand or arm, there was a slight undercurrent. Not static electricity, but some kind of energy that drew your attention to her.

By now, I'm super cautious about everything—what I say, what I do, what I document. I introduce myself and explain why I'm there and then begin to do an initial evaluation. **She says to me, this patient I've never met before, "I've been waiting for you,**

Charlotte. You have so much to give, but you just need to open up yourself more so that people can connect to who you are."

Maybe you can imagine what's going through my mind. She doesn't know me at all and has never met me before. Delusional? Reaction to her medicine? Was someone else talking about me with her? Her comments made me stop and pause. That moment where you're rationalizing what's going on as wrong and crazy, defending yourself, but also the little seed of truth has germinated somewhere. That seed we don't see or believe. It's hiding from us, secretly growing until it sprouts aboveground and we can see it.

Thelma, that's her name, is elderly, frail, less than five feet tall. Her lungs consumed with a disease that prevents her from breathing with the ease we all enjoy. Her life, as a black woman in the south, was difficult. Her life spanned segregation to integration. Later in life, she was allowed to have cleaning jobs for very meager wages. She had a big family with lots of tragedy, but also enormous love and support. She was quietly wise, and the kind of person who doesn't say much, but when she does, everyone around her hangs on every letter of every word. She speaks with intent and lives with a greater purpose.

Somehow, I absorbed this scene I was in, without really understanding it, and sat down in the chair beside her bed. "You don't know me," I say to her.

"Honey, you're such a rebel," she replies with a giggle. "It doesn't become you, but you'll learn."

Silence as we stare at each other.

She smiles and takes my hand. "Honey, it's time for my treatment," she says with a cough. That pulls me back into work mode.

Over the next year, Thelma and I connected when she was in the hospital. I found myself looking through the patient list for when she might be back. Not that I was hoping she'd get sick, but looking forward to seeing her. I'd find a way to change my schedule to spend some time in her room, even trading with other employees to work on her floor. Looking back, those conversations were the start of a turning point. Now when I walked into her room, she'd try to smile but always reached out and touched my hand.

Thelma had a way of not saying much, but what she did say was so very profound. With her difficulties breathing, I did most of the talking at the beginning of her visits. She asked things like, "How do you love that person?" or, "How is that action meaningful to you?" Most of the time, I had one of those deer-in-the-headlights looks on my face. Even if I had a terrible response or no response, her questions had a way of making me uncomfortable in my gut. Without understanding, I knew in my deepest fiber of being that I was supposed to be learning something. Slowly, changes started to happen in me. I began to relate more personally to my coworkers. I was more present with friends and family. I truly wanted relationships on a very deliberate level.

The "new me" was working one very normal sunny day with a medium load of patients and a lunch rendezvous scheduled with a new friend. I was paged to the ER in the middle of my rounds and had to drop everything. I walked into the room, and time began to stand still. The patient in the bed had just been brought in by the ambulance and was not breathing. Before I even looked at her face, I knew it was Thelma. The only thing I can say is that my training took over. That learned ability to bury the emotion and focus on the emergency, the patient who wasn't breathing. She had no identification, but I offered up her name and the name of her physician, who was also very close to her. The team in the room did what we do in those situations, but she didn't make it.

It wasn't until I was at home alone that evening, that I allowed myself to process what had happened and what I had lost. Ultimately, what I had gained in this relationship with Thelma and what I was going to do as a result.

Soon, I changed careers outside of healthcare. I married a wonderful man, and we have a family. In the next sixteen years at Kraft Foods, I grew in experience and in responsibility. I sought out personal development, and in time, passed those learnings on to teams I built. Always a bit of a rebel, I was given opportunities to use that strength in many ways: developing technologies, new products or product improvements, bringing siloed parts of the organization together for a common purpose, creating best practices and teaching the organization how to adopt them, and creating a clear path out of a very complex problem.

Beyond the work you are known for are those things you stand for. You do these things because of how important they are to you. No one has a business goal to better someone's life. People don't remember what you do; they remember how you make them feel and how you connect with them. Each person and each connection is different. This is how Thelma periodically popped back into my life, and her words reminded me and guided me.

At my farewell event from Kraft, I looked across the faces of those with whom I'd spent much of my waking hours. Those faces and lives I knew well. I knew what they wanted, wished for, loved, and hated. I knew their pains and struggles and had been with them to celebrate successes. We had tension in our relationships; they had grown and changed, and so had I.

Every single person felt compelled to share their story of how I'd impacted their lives in front of everyone else. I knew the story, but they wanted others to know.

"She pushed me outside of my comfort zone and challenged me to think differently."

"She helped me to see what I could become, which was great since I didn't see it."

"I wasn't sure I wanted to go that route in my career. I thought it was too risky, but it's turned out to be the best decision."

"She really cared beyond me as an employee, but truly me as a person and a parent."

"There were some things I needed to change if I wanted to have more influence. I was great at innovation. She worked with me and truly supported me through it all."

"She helped me see how I could be me in my work. Be authentic."

It struck me. I'd become Thelma for these people. It wasn't something that was part of my responsibilities, but what I was called to do. I helped them see things about themselves that allowed them to grow and become better versions of who they already were: successful Rebel leaders. I had become the leader that Thelma predicted.

You can, too.

CHAPTER TWO

REBEL UNWRAPPED

"Rebels and non-conformists are often the
pioneers and designers of change."
—Indira Gandhi

Have you ever been that person who tried a new way of doing something? Maybe you saw a way to solve a problem that no one else did. Maybe you wanted to create a future that was a better place. Have you ever created or invented something that didn't exist before? Initially, some people thought you were a little crazy. Was it hard to get support for your ideas or inventions? Did that make you stop, or did you keep going?

From a very young age, we all have instincts on how to do things. We experiment, learn, and then develop opinions about how things should be done. As we get to our professional lives and careers, we gain knowledge and expertise in an area. It's this expertise that allows us to think of ways to improve or change our work or environment.

There are some people who acted on their visions of the future who have created light bulbs, running water, television, internet, air travel, factory automation, smartphones, and space travel.

Then there are those leaders who inspire us by breaking social and cultural barriers. For these individuals, it's intolerable to maintain the status quo and continue the injustices that have been suffered by many for so long. They will risk much to affect the change that's needed. They seem fearless in the face of opposition.

When in the midst of an insurmountable problem, there are people who seem to be able to find a path in the proverbial woods. A way out. A way through. A way forward. These people are determined to figure it out, and they never see "failure" but use experiences as either additional "information" or a stepping stone to a solution.

When needing support for their ideas, solutions, they are very good at influencing others to support them. They have a large network. Perhaps more importantly, a very diverse network of people they reach out to at some frequency to "bounce off ideas" and get feedback. They get money for undeveloped ideas and never seem swayed by hearing "no." Conventional markers of success are very familiar, and they are masters at selling.

This is the Rebel.

CHAPTER THREE

GO FOR IMPACT

Years ago, my friend Vicki was telling me about this crazy idea to move hospital and medical charting to an electronic format. No more paper records or mountains of paper storage. She knew I was working in hospitals part-time, so she was looking for my opinion. This was a big change from what everyone was used to, and the security concerns were significant. How would the patient information remain confidential? What if it got lost? But, wow—not having to read the doctor's handwriting was pretty brilliant. We often had to call and confirm orders over the phone just because of bad handwriting. Her dad had a medical disability and was not able to stand and lift very much, but he was very good with computers. He'd been working on this system and programming for a couple of years. He was ready to start talking to doctor's offices and hospitals about the purchase of the system.

It all starts with ideas, new ways of doing things, and how the future might be created.

"Let's be status quo like we've always been, and just like everyone else," said no successful leader, ever!

Rebels are passionate about their view of the future, especially when they're told their idea isn't possible. Tell any Rebel, "There's no way" or "It can't be done." They will be thinking. "I'll show you just how to do it." Their resolve is strengthened, and there is little fear of obstacles that are placed in their path.

It's not an "only my way" approach either. Successful Rebels keep their eyes on their ultimate vision and the impact they want to achieve. They are persistent and get input from others to build and expand on their ideas. Most importantly, they learn from their opposition because it's not about the idea; it's about the impact.

> *"Avoid brand arrogance. Be the kind of people*
> *other companies want to partner with."*
> —*Harry Epstein, CEO, Quadrant MC*

As a leader with passionate Rebels on your team, you don't need to remind them, track them, or micromanage them. Energy will drive and motivate the team to places the leader can't imagine. The leader needs to be up to the challenge in order to shape the path, develop their team, and rekindle motivation. A leader also needs the flexibility to move the company in a different direction quickly to be successful.

As a Rebel leader, you attract those people who want to be on the team and moving to an exciting new place. The team feeds off the energy of the leader, and together, there's the potential of reaching new heights. High-potential talent is drawn to leaders who are movers and shakers.

CHAPTER FOUR

FAMOUS REBELS

Throughout history, there are many successful people who have affected change and have done it fearlessly and against the odds and opposition. I've listed a few below to illustrate the specific Rebel Characteristics as examples.

It's easy to see these famous people from their point of success. If we read about their fame and fortune from the perspective of where they started, then we see the odds they faced and the obstacles they overcame. These successful people all have characteristics of Rebel leaders.

Oprah: Influential talk show host, author, philanthropist, actress, and media personality. From her early beginnings in poverty and abuse, *The Oprah Winfrey Show* has proved to be one of the most successful and highly watched TV shows of all time—a first for a black female. She is also the first black female billionaire.

Steve Jobs: Co-founder of Apple; smart but directionless and rebelled against formal education until dropping out. The startup began in his parents' garage and was partially funded by the sale of his VW bus. He is recognized as an inventor, designer, and entrepreneur whose revolutionary products, which include the iPod, iPhone, and iPad, are now seen as dictating the evolution of modern technology.

Mother Theresa: Nobel Peace Prize recipient for her humanitarian work. Her order established a hospice; centers for the blind, aged and disabled; and a leper colony. Her "do it anyway commandments" guide many who are mistreated toward a noble "take the high road" response, a radical approach when the typical human response is to retaliate.

Elvis Presley: an American singer and actor. Regarded as one of the most significant cultural icons of the twentieth century, he is often referred to as the King of Rock and Roll. He was one of the first white artists to bring the sound of black musicians to a broader audience, dissolving a barrier thought to be insurmountable.

Tiger Woods: Woods is widely regarded as one of the greatest golfers in the history of the sport, and as one of the most famous athletes of all time. He broke barriers for African-American golfers in a largely white male sport. Tiger's career is most often characterized by the work ethic that propelled him to new heights despite virtually everyone doubting his abilities and stated vision.

It's easy to look at someone's career and see the successes but miss all the hardships, failures, and fear they had to overcome to succeed in their life's endeavors.

CHAPTER FIVE

POWER OF THE REBEL

In many ways, these famous, influential people rebelled against the status quo, challenged the norms, and provided creative solutions and paths previously not seen. **Leaders today want the output that Rebel individuals bring.** Would you say no to creative solutions or societal change or sustained innovation? Why aren't more leadership training classes talking about Rebels? Why aren't hiring practices looking for the Rebel?

You may wonder what those characteristics are that Rebels either need or need to develop. Are they born this way, or can individuals be developed to become more successful at Rebel traits? Does everyone have these traits?

"To obtain success requires a lot of effort and requires a lot of self-reflection and courage to continue with the path that you have set out for yourself."
—*Maria Velissariou, Chief Science and Technology, Institute of Food Technology*

Gregory Berns, neuroscientist and author of *Iconoclast*, finds that "most people's brains are just not wired to go against what everybody else is doing." Our brains look for what's comfortable. After all, that's where the fight-or-flight response resides. Unknown and uncomfortable situations usually result in a physical response of elevated heart rate, rapid breathing, perspiration, and upset stomach. These are all physical symptoms that teach us to avoid situations.

Berns says the challenge is that iconoclastic thinking (doing what others say is impossible) requires higher levels of perception, a different fear response, and social intelligence.

Harvard Business School professor Francesca Gino is an expert on the psychology of organizations and author of *Rebel Talent*. "It pays to break the rules at work and in life." In her research on talented Rebels, she finds they fight against convention and train their minds to avoid stereotypes. **Gino argues that the future belongs to the Rebel and that there's a Rebel in each of us.**

Through my research, experiences, and interviews of entrepreneurs and leaders, I have developed these four main characteristics that describe Rebels well.

1. Innovator: Highly creative thinkers (conceptualize) and doers (bring concepts to life); tends to become immersed in a seemingly impossible situation; with time and thorough

assessment, they are able to see a vision of an elegant and simple solution; a new future state.

2. Explorer: Loves discovery and learning; seeks a range of inputs to form opinions and direction, including those seemingly contrary, or against, their own; seemingly wired and comfortable going against conventional beliefs or norms; some see this as fearless.

3. Invincibles: Rise to the challenge when others don't believe in them; they are comfortable digging into the details to find solutions; in fact, when told something can't be done, that excites them and adds fuel to their motivation; persistent, determined, disciplined.

4. Influencer: Highly tuned relationship and communication skills to influence others for support; able to articulate the value of an idea versus just the technical details; they maintain and leverage their network and are connected to other networks; very savvy with conventional requirements of success and can use that advantageously for unconventional ideas.

Rarely does one person possess strengths in all of these areas. Typically, a person Is strong in one or two of these areas, and when they reach a challenge, they will need to understand which of the four areas may require development or support.

CHAPTER SIX

TRANSLATING THE UNCONVENTIONAL

We had recently moved into our house, and as newlyweds, we were eager to do some fun new projects. My wonderful and handy husband was excited about each new home improvement project as an opportunity to purchase new tools to get the job done. We had the correct tools, directions, and the wood for the crown molding. Scott's an engineer, so plans were identified and needed to be followed. Every time he cut the corner pieces and put them up on the wall, the angles didn't connect as they should. There was always one of the boards that were at the wrong angle or didn't connect the way it was supposed to. He reviews the instructions and repeats the cuts again and again.

I'm watching and listening and trying to be helpful. When finally, he had had enough, I asked if we could try something.

"I've tried everything, and the directions don't seem to work."

"Let's ignore those, then. I think I have this figured out."

You can imagine how well that was received. Almost like blasphemy when you tell an engineer to ignore the directions. **My rationale was if they weren't working, we could ignore them.**

He humors me and cuts small pieces to my instructions and climbs the ladder to the corner of the room. It works! *Isn't that wonderful?* I'm thinking. Now we can finish the project. The look on his face tells a different story. His face was not happy, relieved, or excited.

"How did you do that? Why don't these directions work? They are supposed to."

To me, it didn't matter, and I would have probably shredded those directions because they weren't important to me. Then I thought about who was really going to be installing the crown molding—not me. Did I really want to be *that* involved?

When you put up crown molding, the corner cuts are very tricky and super important. There are two ways to read the instructions: with the long part of the wall as the reference or with the corner of the room as the reference. Once I saw how to make my intuitive understanding fit the directions, all was well in our house. My husband was happy and very independently capable of the job.

Sometimes it takes the Rebel to see the unconventional approach. Sometimes the Rebel also needs to translate that approach to the team. Putting up crown molding needed to be simple and reproducible, and my intuition wasn't going to be available at all times. The translation became critical for the other rooms of crown molding in our house.

PART TWO

REBEL SUCCESS SECRETS

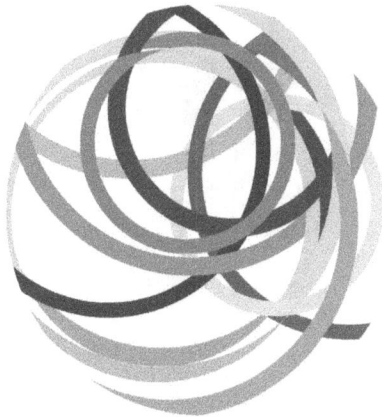

CHAPTER SEVEN

THE PROFIT FACTOR

"In any business, if you're executing the same playbook year after year, you're guaranteed to lose ground to the competition, and it's even more critical in today's digital age because consumer preferences are changing at an exponential rate."
—John Lazowski, VP Marketing, Ingredion

Being a Rebel can be a fun, break-all-the-rules kind of life, living without many boundaries. Similar to many people, they are good at working to their strengths, breaking new ground, testing possibilities, and innovating solutions.

At their core, Rebels want to make a difference, improve a situation, or solve a problem.

THE REBEL WHY

To fully realize their true impact on society, the Rebel needs success. When you only play in the world of accepted convention, success (money, status) can still happen. There's something different about an unconventional, seemingly crazy idea that connects the individual at a deeper level. Personal investment and dedication show up.

Having strong Rebel traits is put to good use when generating success. Without success, it's useless, exhausting, and ineffective. It seems initially counterintuitive, but the real need is for a disciplined Rebel.

Being a Rebel *plus* being successful is so much more satisfying!

Success is measured by a standard. Has a difference been made in lives? Is there commanding market share, exponential revenues, dominating athletic performance, or achieving heights previously not seen by your social or cultural group? There is an internal component to success or self-satisfaction as it's often described. However, success is primarily measured by numbers and includes things like being first, holding the record, number of lives saved, largest revenue.

To be successful, you need to be strong in sales along the way and others need to be interested and receptive to hearing your idea. Even before the idea becomes real and is able to be seen, touched or worked with, you'll need to sell its potential, what it might do. Once it's developed and ready for the end user or consumer, the impact of your idea follows a sale to someone who sees the value and wants to purchase! If you are selling the idea of change and trying to garner support, you are still selling a benefit or improved way of being.

"To be the best in your area of expertise it's critical for leaders to connect authenticity, trust, and a deep sense of responsibility and privilege. These are the principles that endure with time and nature."
—Maria Velissariou, Chief Science and Technology, Institute of Food Technology

Society and business today set these parameters that seem at direct odds to the Rebel leader whose instinct it is to go against the norms. Pairing the two, Rebel and Success, is a delicate balance. The goal is to have an impact on people and/or society through the combination of great ideas with a great balance sheet.

The challenges of pairing Rebel and Success are illustrated in the table with the opposing perspectives frequently held by those who are in one or the other.

Rebel	Success
Internally generated	Externally measured
Unconventional, strives for unique	Uses conventional measures
Unexpected	Predictable
Messy	Disciplined
Not focused, off the rails	Bogged down in detail, loss of creativity

Going back to the successful leader examples, every person understood both elements enough to create impact. In hindsight, they built, developed, and obtained skills and support that were required in order to realize their vision.

People

Building a team is a delicate balance between the two elements. The instinct is to have one person strong in each. This is often very difficult because there's not a translation mechanism. The creatives don't speak balance sheet and vice versa. This can be disastrous for any team. Even if the leader can provide the translation, it's a time-consuming endeavor. The best approach is to find team members with strength in one area and ability or potential in another.

Here is what John Lazowski, VP of Marketing, Ingredion, shares on this subject:

My leadership style in business was greatly influenced by playing for years as a lead guitarist in a rock band. When you play with a group of five to six people who need to work together to create one piece of music, it's important to know when to take the lead and when to let someone else take the lead. The whole idea of improvising when something goes wrong in front of an audience and how that relates to having a vision in business but not knowing all the paths to get there. Creativity and innovation are fragile, and both music and business showed me how important it is to create an environment that fosters imagination.
—Excerpt from an interview with John
Lazowski, VP Marketing, Ingredion

Careers are not straight lines, and organizational structures don't need to be, either. People development enriches experiences and should be the starting point for all leaders. Look for those people with an aptitude for balance, even where a person has a predominant strength in one area. Curiosity to learn new skills is optimal, even if the assignment or timeframe is short. The best result is when the desired endpoint can be linked to a purpose or "why."

CHAPTER EIGHT

FIND AND UNLEASH YOUR REBEL TALENT

Finding yourself, your team, or your organization in any of the following situations may mean you need to find or develop Rebel talent:

- Slow to adopt new ideas

- Not relevant

- Out of business due to competition

- Lacking in diverse ideas

- Comfortable in the norms

- "We've always done it this way" syndrome

It's uncomfortable to be the person in the room speaking up against a particular idea. Going against the grain has lost more than one person their job, particularly when it's something the leader doesn't agree with. It's also true that there are numerous examples of when that one idea was shared, then built upon, then developed, then sold in market. That one idea, given air time, becomes the difference-maker, the impact-generator, and the market leader.

Sharing your idea for a new business, product, service can also be uncomfortable, if not scary. How many times have those fledging ideas been shot down before they have a chance to grow? Not being able to answer *all* the questions about your idea, can keep us from sharing even the beginnings of one.

I recall a time early in my career when the company was going through some difficult challenges. There was a lot of leadership focus on the problem, and "new thinking" was required. I was so excited to offer my perspective as I thought there had to be a couple of possible solutions to this problem. When we got to the meeting to discuss the possible solutions, I was so excited to offer really great ideas that stretched boundaries, new thinking. After I offer the suggestions, dead silence—not a single word. I saw looks given to my boss, like *why was she invited?* I felt like I had done something wrong by suggesting an idea and a possible solution.

The few people who are comfortable being Rebels are able to generate ideas and have them flourish. They seek support and input to their ideas regardless of the response they receive. There's a "do it anyway" mentality. The more mature Rebels recognize that even the negative feedback they receive is important in refining their idea and ultimately getting support.

"Meet people where they are, help them thrive from where they are, and understand their motivations."
—Stephanie Chedid, President and CEO, Luther Manor

The majority of people who, according to Burns, "are just not wired to go against what everybody else is doing," can have great ideas, often really good ones since they've spent a lot of time thinking them over. Diversity of thought and contribution produces the best, simplest, and most efficient ideas and solutions. The challenge for every individual is to recognize where they are. The challenge for every leader is to recognize where their team is and, when given the opportunity to build a team, to create that diversity and spectrum of Rebel talent.

LEVEL UP*

Think of the people you know and those who seem to have strong Rebel Characteristics. Describe someone you think is a Rebel and then use that example to consider how you can grow to a new level of success personally.

- List three traits you admire in that person

- List three traits you believe you personally have

- List three traits you would like to become better at

---

* All Level Up activities can be found in the Appendix

Rebels aren't the type to sit and wait idly for direction. They will be looking at options on their own and experimenting on the side, trailblazing new ground.

> *"We need thinkers at every level. We need*
> *people to pivot and evolve."*
> —Stephanie Chedid, President and CEO, Luther Manor

As a leader, you may not be crystal clear with what's needed to change the situation. Often you do have a very clear understanding that the current set of circumstances is undesirable and unsustainable.

The pressure may be on the rise at the office. The team is underperforming. Cuts are needed to balance the budget and return value to shareholders. The organization you work with may find it difficult to attract volunteers or find support for its programs. Funding is short, and when it's available, it doesn't seem to come your way.

Reviews haven't been going well. The regular hints and comments from your manager are becoming more frequent. The expectations of your performance have changed. The market dynamics have shifted, and your team or company has been slow to adapt. There are skills you know you need, but you just haven't had the time to dedicate to obtain and perfect those skills. This role may no longer hold the same appeal for you, and there may be no foreseeable growth.

Here is the approach one managing director takes:

"We are system thinkers, so we are looking for people who can think critically and creatively and bring new ideas for new opportunities to others across the organization."
—Bridget Croke, Managing Director, Closed Loop Partners

There are two main approaches to use in this situation. Find what you're looking for from the outside (build) or from the inside (develop). The next section covers the basics of how to do both.

Build a New Team

A phenomenal opportunity for any leader is to add new talent to the group, team, or organization. Who you hire reflects on your leadership abilities, and being a good talent scout is a desirable characteristic of any leader. When done well, it can be a very quick way to adjust the course. When done poorly, it's a humongous waste of time.

Build Success Story

I started working with a team that had key openings. The challenge was that the new hires didn't stay more than the first three months. The leader was super frustrated at the wasted efforts and wasn't sure how to fix it. This had happened three times in the past year. Not only were they not retaining new hires, but they weren't able to get their first choice talent in the first place.

The shift was pretty simple but required a new way of thinking. This company, in general, had the perspective that anyone would want to work for them, and they had the best pick of the talent. The issue was what had worked for years was no longer working. Jobs are plentiful, and applicants realize they are spending a huge part of their waking hours at a job. More and more frequently, people are making decisions about where they spend their time based on whether they feel valued at a given company or organization. After all, doesn't everyone want to feel valued?

Once this team shifted to marketing the benefits of the role to the candidate—what they would gain, learn, develop, etc.—their candidate pool increased not only in numbers but in quality of candidate. They were already conducting phone and onsite interviews, but they shifted how they exposed the candidate to their company and culture. This was no cost to the company versus what they were doing currently but took time since it was a big cultural shift for them.

In the end, they filled the slots with great candidates, and their new-hire retention hit their goals.

How do you adjust the process to find, onboard, and success-fully launch new talent, and do that successfully within the exist-ing environment? This can feel very overwhelming and impossible, but I'd recommend starting with the specific details below.

1. **Change how you search.** You're looking for people who love to move mountains with success. No matter how big or small you think your specific mountain is, you need to make it interesting. Changing how the job description is written, how the role is marketed, and how the role is interviewed for are all critical for success.

   Here is what one CEO shares about what they look for:

   "I hire for aptitude and attitude. One is
   as important as the other to me."
   —Natalie Lamberton, CEO, *Talas Harbor Healthcare*

   a. **Job description** (JD): sit down with the original descrip-tion that you would have always written, a printout of the four main Rebel Characteristics, and a second version of the JD that is at least triple spaced, so there's room to write in between the lines. Choose at least three places within the expectations where you can add some of the Rebel verbiages. Also, look to the competencies or skills demonstration area and choose or edit so that you have one to three that are specific to the Rebel talent.

b. **Marketing the role**: There's typically a section at the beginning that tells them about your company and specifics on the part of the organization, group, or team that the role is being hired into. This is an opportunity to speak to the person you want to hire. You write this section for them. *Why* should they apply to this role? The second place you market is when you advertise for the role— either on one of the popular search engines like LinkedIn or Indeed, or with a recruiter. The recruiter will speak about the role on your behalf and sell the role to potential candidates. It's useful to create two to five sentences that market the opportunity of using some of the key Rebel Characteristics that are important for this role.

c. **Interviewing**: Depending on the size of your company, you either have a highly structured process or a less formal one. Every single person who speaks to this candidate will not only be assessing the candidate but in a position to successfully market the role and your company. Make sure they all understand what the strategy is with this hire. You can't adjust the JD and the marketing but leave the interviewing the same. How can you use the interviews to showcase to the candidate the value this role will bring to the organization? Get a read on the new Rebel Characteristics that interest you. How have they demonstrated those in the past?

"Lead with a small ego. Senior leaders need to fit the culture, and how you do something is the bigger factor."
—Kathy Bolhous, CEO, Charter NEX and Next Generation Films

2. Set up the new hire/transfer for success, onboarding, mentors, etc.

Now you have a talented new person who will come into the group or organization with a new way of thinking and a new way of doing things. This is most successful if you think of this as a two-way onboarding. Both the new person acquiring the required role-based knowledge and the existing team or group will learn from the new person.

As a leader, put the steps in place and set the expectations for the team receiving a new member. It's best they have three different connection points and ideally three different people. The GSD (get stuff done) person is the one who knows how things work, who to go to, where to find what you're looking for. The skills person is for specific onboarding related to projects and systems. The mentor person is the one they can go to for culture-related questions. The mentor can be difficult to assign, as that is a bit more trust-based, so what I recommend is to set up meetings and/or lunches between the new person and the existing team.

When the new person has a team, it's important to set up a new leader assimilation activity to delve into the interpersonal aspects of how the new leader interacts with the team.

3. The leader must set the stage for the upcoming change.

When the leader is bringing in new team members with the objective of bringing new thinking to the team, it's critical that the leader goes through the steps to prepare the current team. This is best done multiple months in advance. Important aspects that should be covered are current situation (gaps, needs, need to fill outside, describe the vision of the future), how this supports the need for the new hire, and how the current team can support their role in the change and the onboarding of the new person.

LEVEL UP*

Depending on where you are, focus on one main area and list two potential things you, as the leader, could do differently to support the change that is needed.

- Two criteria to add to a new team member search

- Two elements to consider adding to an onboarding process

- Two actions you can take to set the stage for the upcoming change.

---

* All Level Up activities can be found in the Appendix

Develop New Teams

Most leaders don't have the ability to hire to build a team, and in these cases, the focus is on the development of the existing team. It starts with an assessment of self and team and an individual conversation with each team member about the situation, the assignment expectations, and their aspirations. From here, there any number of directions the conversation could lead. Development conversations should be at least quarterly and completely separate from a project or strategy specific conversation.

"One of our most important secrets for talent are the four As: Authentic, Approachable, Accountable, and Action-oriented."
—Kathy Bolhous, CEO, Charter NEX and Next Generation Films

We, as leaders, are often surprised when team members have unexpected gifts or unarticulated desires to grow. Who knew? Sometimes the employee themselves has been working to others' expectations for so long they are unaware of their own strengths. Everyone works best within their strengths and focuses on their specific opportunity areas that have become barriers to career progress. These conversations are great opportunities to connect an individual's goals and objectives to the areas of development. Use the goals as vehicles to demonstrate new development and growth.

LEVEL UP*

- Using the four Rebel traits of innovator, explorer, invincible, influencer, consider two current team members and what might they do differently.

- Where might they have underdeveloped potential? Where might you provide stretch opportunities?

- What are the ways you'll have the conversation with them about the potential you see and how you'd like to encourage it?

---

* All Level Up activities can be found in the Appendix

CHAPTER NINE

GO OFF-ROAD FOR BEST RESULTS

"As long as we have the talent, we have the technology."
—Yan Ke, CTO Clobotics

Have you ever been given any of this feedback?

- Be clearer on where you want to go

- The team doesn't understand your vision

- Your ideas seem all over the place; people can't follow you

- We never hear from you in a meeting

- What happened to that idea you were working on?

- You need to speak up more

- That meeting wasn't the right time to bring that up

- To be successful at the next level, you need to learn to influence

- How will you fund that? Money doesn't grow on trees

Feedback is always a gift, even when receiving it doesn't feel the same as getting flowers or a new watch. Now that you have the feedback, what do you do with it? That's the challenge of the leader—defining the desired outcome and putting the steps in place to get there.

Defining the desired outcome can be as straightforward as taking the list of bullet points above, or substituting ones you've heard personally, and writing out the statement you'd prefer to hear. The below table illustrates some examples.

From	To
We never hear from you in a meeting	Your input was valuable
Your ideas seem all over the place; people can't follow you	I can clearly understand the logic of how those ideas come to life.
Be clearer on where you want to go	The team understands and is excited about your vision
To be successful at the next level, you need to learn to influence	Wow, you were able to get resources to further your idea. Great job!

The source(s) needs to be identified accurately and, in my experience, tends to come from one of three areas: team, individual, organization. Most often, there's more than one area that needs attention.

TEAMS

How do you diagnose if the solution needs to come from the team?

- Is it what the team looks like? Do you need different members?

- Is it how the team operates, behaves, and works together?

A diverse team has the best chance of a unique solution. Ideas need input from multiple sources to be successful. An idea can start as a fledgling and grows when built upon and added to. An idea that pushes the boundaries of convention and is successful will be a team effort. How do you put the team together to be successful?

"It's the fearlessness of saying, 'I know people have done it this way, but I'm going to question absolutely everything I see about it.' Reassemble the ideas in new ways, take away things, add new things, and fearlessly move forward."
—*Harry Epstein, CEO, Quadrant MC*

If you are in a position to create the desired team, think about each contributor on at least two dimensions: their area of specific expertise the team needs, and their unique personal contribution (UPC). Some refer to this as the "soft skill," but these UPCs are significant contributions to team success. Your team needs to be made up of individuals with distinctly different UPCs, and the members need to understand that you find value in the contribution of their UPC. When evaluating members on their UPC contributions, it's useful to ask yourself if this person has a view of the world or of things that would add a valuable perspective to this team.

The top UPC skill to have on your team is someone who is good at translation. Who can translate marketing to production or sales to research? Or, who has experience putting together a nonlinear supply chain in computer hardware and can assist on a supply-chain project in a different industry? Strong breadth is another term used to describe this skill.

In what seemed like overnight, we are facing a pandemic that has had the vast majority of people around the globe at home sheltering in place or under super strict quarantines. Whoever your "team" was, that structure is pretty much gone. Your work colleagues, your school friends, your moms groups, church organizations, sports teams—the ability to meet and continue building those relationships, shut down. Many of us quickly learned how to become much better at connecting virtually to maintain relationships and connections.

But what about the home team? If you didn't live alone, all of a sudden, for weeks at a time, you were with people 24/7 and needed to learn to live like a team with your family. Characteristics that may have been tolerable for a couple of hours in the evening became suddenly unbearable. And you can't get away from them because you're stuck at home! While we may have learned to work with diverse work, school, or volunteer groups, we've not learned to work or live with our diverse family members.

In extreme circumstances, diverse teams become super powerful. There is a singular focus around a goal and a common understanding. Each team member's role is clear. The team flexes when challenges shift and often emerge greater. **So, here's some of what we did as a family and what we learned:**

- **Transparency.** Daily gratitude became even more important. It was an existing practice for us as a family to offer two gratitudes and one screw-up during dinner. Gratitudes remind us that there's always something to be grateful for. The screw-ups statements started when our son kept saying that he was the only one who was getting in trouble or doing anything wrong. I realized that he never saw the things we screwed up at work or how we adjusted as a result. Some examples: my husband lost his entire work hard drive; we had no clean dishes one night because I hadn't run the dishwasher; my son took a tight turn on his bike too fast and gouged his knee. How does this work in a professional environment? Transparency with your team is critical.

- **Schedule.** A household schedule was established with designated project time, individual time, and exercise. Project time allowed everyone to feel as though they accomplished something. The individual time allowed that downtime that everyone needed. The exercise was super important in keeping us healthy and reducing stress.

- **Cleaning.** A few of the key messy areas.

- **Defined workspaces for everyone.** This was super important for everyone. My husband and I already worked from home. The addition of our son required a shift. He got an upgraded bedroom out of it. I got a converted guest room to accommodate my office. I was really a nomad before—anywhere there was internet. With my places to work limited, I needed a defined place with a door that could be shut.

- **Schedule shift.** We all had to shift our schedules a bit to accomplish work and school. It was important to have an adult available for schoolwork questions. A structure was set up to monitor break times and ensure there was exercise during the day.

There are two big takeaways that are emerging from this experience for us as a family. The ability for us to model behaviors to each other was key. Each of us learned something from the other's experience. The other key takeaway was valuing our teenager's very different contributions. We were the adults and had a learned set of behaviors, and he was the kid, so he was the

different one. We learned to incorporate those diverse contributions and become a stronger team.

*"Aspects of leadership are vital in today's world, especially
as employees want more of an ethical alignment and
almost a responsibility of the corporation back to them."*
—James Stephens, CEO, Blue Marble Biomaterials

LEVEL UP*

Consider a successful team you've been a part of or led.

- What were the key components of success for that team?

- Were there best practices you learned in that experience and continue to use?

_____

* All Level Up activities can be found in the Appendix

BEST PRACTICES FOR SUCCESSFUL TEAMS:

As you think about the professional environment, the transparency we used at home is still critically important as you create that ethical alignment with the individual and the corporation. It connects to how the individual values their contribution. The selection of team members is another critical aspect. **I have found the best success is with a diverse team that can bring up and discusses diverse ideas, including contrary perspectives.**

- How do you work with and develop the team to get the desired output? For any team, the key components of the process are pretty straightforward, listed below. There are, of course, many detailed steps that are included and some unique elements that are specific to the team or the company.
  - Development of an idea
  - Determination to stick with it
  - Influence, present, and/or translate to others

These are steps that are important for all ideas, including the conventional ones, but we at Rebel Success specialize in the unconventional for exceptional results! So, what are the differences?

Rebel Success Practices

- **When we consult with clients to develop ideas, we deliberately use methods that seek tension.** How you balance both the developing and nurturing of an idea, as well as fully understanding its flaws and why it won't go forward. Many ideation session activities lean heavily on the develop-and-nurture side. Almost all groups or teams become emotionally attached during this process. Ideas should be built and nurtured enough so they can be clearly understood and communicated. Any gaps, and there will be gaps, need to be understood early. Seeking the tension means the team needs to be uncomfortable unless they've done a true assessment of the gaps in their idea. Why won't someone like it? Why won't it succeed?

- **Stick-with-it-ness.** Can you evaluate the potential of an idea to deliver something new? Is there an early-stage prototype or concept that can be tested? Teams need to understand how to get to this stage and that perfection is not the goal. It's easy to give up, especially in the wake of negativity and failures. Teams should view failures as development direction.

- **Influence is supercritical.** The team has invested efforts in features, functions, and the *how* of things. To influence well, they need to concentrate on benefits and *why*. Within a company or organization, that often requires translation to another functional language like marketing and sales. Has the team been built for this skill? A lob over the fence is rarely successful.

INDIVIDUALS

It all begins with self-awareness. As a leader, if you don't see the results you want, do a self-evaluation. If you've been given feedback, try to pinpoint your words or nonverbal actions that are at the crux. Do you see yourself exhibiting the traits strongly enough to get the results you want? If not, an evaluation of where you are versus where you want to be is in order. To get started, assess whether your challenges are mostly in one of these three areas: generating ideas, developing them further, or selling or influencing others.

> *"Leaders need to connect authenticity and trust, a deep sense of responsibility, and the privilege to be the best in an area of expertise. For me, these are the principles that are enduring with time."*
> —Maria Velissariou, CS&T, Institute of Food Technology

ORGANIZATIONS

Organizational success will rely on culture to a certain degree. Culture can be challenging but not impossible. I'll cover it briefly with an example, but the Rebel Success team approaches the challenges of culture individually.

The tale of two projects:

My team was working very closely with another team in the company. There were two top projects that had been challenging for years. Both involved changing an iconic product to be more aligned with consumer trends. The structure was one lead per team per project. and we thought the structure created the environment for the co-leads to work in a new way unencumbered by prior obstacles. Project 1 was a market success and the iconic product grew. Project 2 took almost an additional year to get off the ground and was a much slower path to completion.

The difference boiled down to culture. Project 2 had a lead that wasn't open to new ideas or to test out new solutions—that team's deeply ingrained culture limited success from the beginning.

LEVEL UP*

Determine one to three ideas that you personally as a leader, would like to explore using a new and different approach in the following three areas:

1. Ideas for the organization

2. Ideas for the team

3. Ideas for yourself

---

* All Level Up activities can be found in the Appendix

CHAPTER TEN

BELIEVE IN YOUR REBELS

It was late enough for the sun to have just gone down one evening in early August. My son, Ryan, and a friend were out fishing and determined to catch something before coming in. When they did come in, I heard banging and slamming of doors.

"I know it's here somewhere. She's always rearranging things, but we'll find it," Ryan says.

A few more bangs and slams and I'm downstairs checking it out. Rounding the corner, I hear, "Mom, I need a filet knife." My first thought was, *no, you don't. It's dark, fish are slippery, and your friend hasn't done this before.* But Ryan had this very determined, rebellious look on his face that I'd seen before. He's my rebel. Against my better judgment, I agreed and began to take precautions.

I set them up on the patio with the bucket of fish, a knife, and a piece of wood to cut on. I'm watching them just inside the porch, away from the mosquitoes, and close to the first aid kit. The first place any self-respecting teenager looks for instruction is a YouTube video. Ryan found a few that were funny and pointed out key techniques to follow in others. Once they picked the video with the best instruction, the next search was for music. And an interesting selection of AC/DC and Queen. Finally, they are ready! Ryan had done this before, so he filleted his fish with no problem. Now for his friend's turn. I sit up taller, get closer to the window, and open the first aid kit. Since he hadn't done this before, he was super cautious. It was a very slow process. So slow that I got distracted and stopped paying attention, until I heard a very loud. "Oh my gosh!" As I stand up in alarm, I see a very tiny filet being held up. "I really did it. I didn't think I could, but I just filleted a fish. This is the best sleepover ever!"

Ryan's Rebel approach worked perfectly. Every day, leaders create the future for their companies, organizations, and teams by innovating in ways that challenge accepted norms. Success means seeing a clear path, overcoming those barriers of fear that hold so many people back, and being able to influence others for support. So how can we all start thinking and behaving more like a Rebel? How can we model that behavior to others?

Modeling behavior follows a see-do-teach process. One person watches another perform a task or skill. They then perform that task themselves. The cycle repeats itself when they teach the next person. Since we're talking about behaviors, it's not only about what is being done but more of *how* it's being done that's important. These could be behaviors you are personally good at and would like to model to increase that behavior in someone else. These could also be behaviors you feel you need to develop, and modeling is a way of growing and testing your new skills. Be fearless!

LEVEL UP*

Choose two Rebel behaviors you could model to someone else to advance their skills or development.

- How will you be available to provide feedback as they demonstrate their approach the first time?

- What are the important elements between the two approaches that should be consistent, and what are those elements where there's freedom to change?

---

* All Level Up activities can be found in the Appendix

CHAPTER ELEVEN

DISCOVER YOUR BEST REBEL

No matter where you are in your career or your role in the organization, Rebel Success starts with you. Where do you want to be, and where do you want the team to be?

Self-assess: Where are you versus where you want to be?

Before we get into the details of what makes a Rebel, it's important for you to determine your Rebel Rating.

The four main characteristics of Rebels that I coined and use in my work are detailed below. A person tends to be predominant in one characteristic and less commonly is strong in multiple characteristics. It's rare to be strong in all four.

1. **Innovator**: Highly creative thinkers (conceptualize) and doers (bring concepts to life); tends to become immersed in a seemingly impossible situation; with time and thorough assessment; are able to see a vision of an elegant and simple solution; a new future state.

2. **Explorer**: Loves discovery and learning; seeks a range of inputs to form opinions and direction, including those

seemingly contrary, or against, their own; seemingly wired and comfortable going against conventional beliefs or norms; some see this as fearless.

3. **Invincible**: Rises to the challenge when others don't believe in them; they are comfortable digging into the details to find solutions; in fact, when told something can't be done, that excites them and adds fuel to their motivation; persistent; determined; disciplined.

4. **Influencer**: Highly tuned relationship and communication skills to influence others for support; able to articulate the value of an idea versus just the technical details; they maintain and leverage their network and are connected to other networks; very savvy with conventional requirements of success and can use that advantageously for unconventional ideas.

Using these characteristics is a great way to understand where you are today. We use these definitions and Rebel Rating as one of the early tools when we work with our private clients. If you've purchased *Rebel Success for Leaders*, don't miss the special offer at the end that you can use to take the next step in your personal success.

LEVEL UP*

Below are four questions to get you started. As you consider each question, assess where you are versus where you want to be. Describe the circumstances in detail. What you say, how you feel, what are other people's perspectives of you, what are your thoughts and expectations?

How would you describe your answers to these four questions today?

- Do you enjoy working in the unknown?

- Do you frequently get diverse opinions?

- Do you tackle problems others shy away from?

- Are you good at describing and presenting your ideas to others?

---

* All Level Up activities can be found in the Appendix

In an ideal world, one to three years from now, how would you like to answer these questions? What do you aspire to do differently?

If your answers in one to three years are different from today, how would you bridge that gap? Just one idea is enough to get started. What one thing will you begin doing?

CHAPTER TWELVE

UP YOUR REBEL MAGNETISM

People often ask me how to find successful Rebels for their teams and organizations. You may know a leader or public figure that always seems put together, dressed well for their role, and looks well-rested, not stressed. Without much effort, they attract a following of people who want to learn about them and figure out how to be more like them. **In business and organizations, this is the person whose team you want to be on, the person for whom you want to work. When they speak, people listen. Their opinion carries more weight than almost anyone else on the team.**

So how do you figure this out? Learn to be a magnet so people will be drawn to you. Some would call this leadership presence. You know that special sauce that makes people around you say you're a natural leader and want to be on your team because you have special abilities.

Believe it or not, **it starts with your thoughts.** Thoughts are powerful. I'm not talking about random ideas that pop into your head but rather the complete visualization of a future state: what you want to be, what you want to achieve, and how you will feel when you get there.

Some of the biggest successes in business, sports, and politics credit the law of attraction and visualization to their success.

The law of attraction is the belief that positive thoughts attract positive outcomes while negativity begets negative outcomes. There's science behind the fact that when you think negative thoughts, your body's response, at a biological level, is very similar to fight or flight. Negative thoughts create a response as if you are in danger. Your body tenses, and you begin to behave as if there's an emergency.

> **"Negative is way more contagious than positive,**
> **and it can overtake your organization."**
> —Lori Zindl, President, OS Inc / efficientC Claim Source

We need to be mindful of what we are attracting. Is it serving our goals?

Visualization is a technique where you create a snapshot or picture in your mind of what you want in the future. Basketball players will not only practice their drills and shots on the court, but they will visualize that success in their minds. How the ball arcs to the net, bouncing off the backboard, and how the net moves as the ball goes in. Success is created in their mind, along with how their body is trained to execute the move.

People are attracted to and follow energy and vibrancy. Everyone has a different level of energy they identify with, feel comfortable with, and in which they perform their best. Low energy mode doesn't produce much other than the need for a nap, caffeine, or other stimulants that produce undesirable side effects.

People also want to make a difference, follow their purpose, and make a positive impact on society. This often requires change, doing something out of convention, and creating innovative options and solutions. The energy required to activate change is greater than the energy required to maintain the status quo. This is the challenge and why it's hard to start and maintain this level without burnout. Leaders need to constantly monitor their energy/vibrancy output and reserve to continually attract the talent and support to move their objective forward.

If you are looking to up your magnetism and don't know where to begin, then I suggest starting on one of the three areas listed below. These three areas, in my experience, all need to be true to be a magnetic leader. To attract both the people you need and want as well as the support for your ideas and solutions, think about how you can apply these concepts.

- Be positive in words and actions

- Focus on others: how you listen and demonstrate attention

- Paint a compelling picture of where you're headed

Remember, whether you think this will work or it won't, you're right.

I often start new things as experiments. I read or hear of new concepts or ideas and the ones that interest me, and I try them out. Since I'm also someone who seeks the tension in new ideas, there's also a healthy dose of "why this won't work." The concept of magnetism came along for me right around the time I was launching a speaking business. Speaking or presenting in front of people was familiar to me. Speaking about my brand as a business was a learning curve. So I set off on my experiment to see if I could use this concept of magnetism to attract what I wanted: speaking opportunities at companies and organizations. I wrote down what I wanted and started talking to people about it. I'd casually drop the "speaking idea" in conversation with friends and associates. Then I started talking about it with new people I had just met. I started gathering information and was introduced to an organization for speakers. These pieces and information were how I filled out the vision of the future—a bit like drawing an outline in pencil and then filling it in with color.

Truly, it was amazing how fast it happened, looking at it in retrospect. It's absolutely not a magic wand sort of thing—I did still have to do the work. The doors opened much faster. The connections with the people I've met seemed to align with my objectives. Now I'm a big fan. If you aren't yet, start small but big enough that you don't already have a solution.

LEVEL UP*

Steps for Increasing Your Magnetism

- Assess where you are now. This can be as simple as recording your thoughts or your words. Make a list of how many are positive and how many aren't.

- Then describe what happens when you need something, like achieving a goal, and how you find the people who help you.

- Now, visualize three specific areas you want to be more magnetic (personal or professional).

- Write down two specific sentences you'll begin to speak out loud to others that would increase your magnetism. Maybe you choose something you often say that you'd like to change. The two specific sentences are what you will say in its place.

---

* All Level Up activities can be found in the Appendix

CHAPTER THIRTEEN

HOW TO HAVE LIMITLESS ENERGY

"Energy flows where intention goes."
—*James Redfield*

It's exciting and rewarding to pursue ideas and solutions. Build a team and develop them. Get support for your vision. Make the impact that's rewarding. Rebels love to live this way!. They require a lot of energy to sustain and continue this level of contribution. Not only can this be exhausting for even the most determined Rebel, but burnout is quick to follow. Just doing more to have more impact isn't sustainable. **Rebels need an energy strategy to be successful long term. I'm very passionate about this one and feel it's an often overlooked essential for Rebel Success.**

Burnout can sneak up on even the best of us. We think we can handle it and that it's just temporary. It'll always get better ... later.

I remember when I was at a stressful time in my career. I truly was experiencing burnout. Every day that winter, when I was driving to work, I had an overwhelming urge to go to sleep. Not just the kind where you need thirty more minutes on the clock before the alarm, but the kind where every cell in your body needs more rest and rejuvenation. My drive was only thirty minutes, but I was really worried that I wasn't going to be able to make it to work and stay awake. I looked at myself in the rearview mirror and realized that pudginess was the reason I needed to buy another size up. Other odd things were happening. It seemed my hair was falling out, or at least I was breaking it while brushing. My skin itched in places that didn't use to itch.

I wasn't buying the "you're falling apart" or the "you're getting old" lines. The reality was that the fatigue was overwhelming, and I hadn't seen it sneak up on me. Have you ever heard the story about the frog who doesn't jump out of boiling water because he doesn't notice as the water slowly increases one degree at a time until it dies? I always told myself that I'd figure it out. I realized pretty quickly that drastic changes were needed or the time I wanted to spend with my family, and the impact I wanted to have would be gone.

> *"Scientists call motivation 'activation energy' the force required to get you to change from something you're doing on autopilot to doing something new."*
> —Mel Robbins

Deciding to make the shift is the first step to a better you. Rarely do people stumble into this. It needs to be an intentional effort. Energy flows where intention goes. So I began to break down my challenges into three desirable endpoints. Then the next steps would be to rely on the research I was already familiar with to fill in any gaps.

- Clear head

- Efficiently functioning body

- Family and social connections

Our bodies are perfectly designed systems. They are efficient, effective, embedded with checks and balances, and have the ability to form new pathways and regenerate when needed. Much of our hectic lifestyle, poor eating habits, lack of exercise, and lack of self-care creates imbalance with our biochemistry, neurology and overall well-being. This creates inefficiencies in our bodies and in our minds.

"Setting yourself up to be the best version of yourself through your wellness strategy is so important to really be at the top of your game and make the important decisions."
—*Wendy Horton, Chief Administrative Officer, OSU Wexner Medical Center*

We won't be delving into any biochemistry, don't be concerned. I'm a science geek at heart and love all things related to health, food, and medicine. Personally I have a great deal of passion for this area. The ability to connect our leadership performance to choices and actions we take every day is limitless. This is why it's one of the programs we offer, **Rebel Success: How to find the power, strength, and energy to get everything you want in record time.** I will cover three main focus areas so that you can begin now. Some of you will have heard this before, while to others, the recommendations will be unconventional.

Food

"You can't outrun your fork."
—Unknown

Many people have used exercise to compensate or correct non-optimal food or beverage choices. Those people have had success for a while, but inevitably, over time, this approach stops working. Then we have a list of excuses for why using exercise to compensate for poor food choices is not working. If you've decided that having an enviable system that allows you to think clearly and operate at your best, then you need to figure out food.

I'm only going to recommend three things. These are the three that work for me, and that covers the majority of the guidance any person can find with Google, social media, friends at the gym, or your doctor's office. Once you've read my list below and before you make your list of exceptions and why these things aren't true for you, ask yourself: what do I really want?

1. **Follow an anti-inflammatory approach.** This means to limit or eliminate those food choices that tend to create an inflammatory response in your body. Common culprits are sugar, processed foods, dairy, gluten, and alcohol.

2. **Higher plant-based diet.** There are many ways to eat more plant-based foods these days. The diversity of good stuff in plants can't be beaten: nutrients, micronutrients, fiber, anti-oxidants, etc. Go small, go big, just go and do it.

3. **Manage quantity.** Your body is efficient, and it knows when it's full as long as you can read the memo. The best way to do this is to be in tune with the signals your body is sending you, but very often, the signals are clogged or not getting through. There are many approaches that can't be addressed here, but increasing your self-awareness is a great place to start. How do you feel when you eat something? Are you hungry or just really thirsty? Can you go for twelve hours between dinner and breakfast and only drink water?

Body

Our bodies were created to move. Our spine has designed flexibility. Our muscles are there to be used. Sleep is the designed regenerative time. We weren't made to sit or hunch over devices or spend our days in meetings. Sleeping four hours so we can work more wasn't the designer's recommendation. Those activities consume much of modern life, but we are able to adjust our activities to perform those functions our bodies were made to do.

- **Move regularly.** Walk, run, attend an exercise class (yoga, strength training, circuit training, etc.)

- **Sweat.** Implied in move regularly but important enough to bring out separately. Part of the designed mechanism to get rid of stuff

- **Increase your heart rate.** Also implied in movement and sweat. Activity is great, but the recommendation is for exercise

- **Sleep.** The statistics are staggering and seem to constantly increase. Every age group has trouble sleeping, and the numbers are only increasing. Make it a priority to get seven hours.

Connect

Gets your body out of fight-or-flight mode. Connect to something beyond or bigger than you. This could be nature, higher power, spirit, God, etc. There are a variety of techniques and ways to do this. Whatever your preferred method, it should have the following characteristics:

- **Daily**. Start with a daily amount of time. Five to fifteen minutes even can be beneficial

- **Alone**. This is not something you do with others

- **Still**. It's very unconventional to be still, but that's what it takes

Some of the more common techniques are meditation, either guided or not, praying, journaling, or scripting. This is separate from exercise. "The zone" or the "runner's high" can certainly make us feel connected but comes with an elevated heart rate and rapid breathing.

Feeling like you have limitless energy is possible. Sometimes we stumble upon these practices accidentally, but when purposeful steps are taken, and each of the elements is combined, leaps in success are possible.

CHAPTER FOURTEEN

SELLING AND INFLUENCING

"Everybody lives by selling something."
—*Robert Louis Stevenson*

No matter what your work or your life is about, you're selling something—selling yourself for a job, selling a product or service on the market, even selling the idea of staying out late to your parents. It's a value exchange between two parties or organizations.

As a Rebel, you are living the unconventional, changing the norms. You frequently hear "that can't be done," or, "no one will ever do that," or, "it'll never be successful."

"No" happens almost 100 percent of the time, and the Rebel persists anyway by data gathering, seeking inputs, trial and error, seeking funding for successful project stages, and/or adjusting the idea given the feedback.

The ideas at the early stages are fledgling, raw and not ready to be sold as finished products with all the required elements. In technology or science fields, joint intellectual property creation is a big area of negotiation because the "thing" hasn't been created, but you want to ensure you're set up well for success. Ideas reduced to practice and protected under patent or trade secret law is an entire area of expertise.

At various stages of the process, the sale needs to happen. The potential for an idea will be sold to get development, testing, or support dollars. A product or service will be exchanged for money. Measures of success are very conventional; however, Rebel ideas may not have been created or not fully fleshed out at this stage. The value has not been market-tested. Taking this into consideration, there are a couple of specific areas of selling and influencing that are important and perhaps distinct to Rebel Success.

A big point to remember is that it's rare to find a person equally as good at innovating ideas and being able to influence others to support their ideas. Many options exist in this case: development of skills, pairing a strong innovator with a strong influencer or mentoring, to name a few.

When thinking about how to sell or influence others with your idea or solution, it's important to have a clear idea/concept, define the "why" benefit, and have a clear ask.

Clear idea/concept: The work to gather input from lots of people in your network helps to refine the idea. This includes the inputs from people who don't agree with you. Get some feedback from the person you think would ultimately be your customer. If the value is not clear, you need to rework the idea. Sometimes having a mentor or trusted advisor is valuable in forming the idea if they also have strong skills in this area.

"Why" benefit: Probably the most important part and one you should spend as much time as you need. Teeth whitening is not about white teeth. It's about self-confidence and feeling like you look good in front of a group. The initial instinct may be to convince people on the physical features or attributes, but it's really about the benefit or value to the person or group. The user experience needs to be positive with the product or service. People buy things or pay money for services that make them feel good.

Clear ask: Whatever it is, ask for what you want. Be prepared for the questions and how you may answer them. If it's money, what's it for, and how will you know if the work is successful? If you are looking for non-monetary support, influence and introductions give some thought to what you may offer in exchange. The best position is to have already given thought to what you can offer before you make an ask. Be clear and strong in voice. Confidence equates to your belief. If the other person senses your belief wavering, then they question their support. Then be quiet! There's nothing worse than making the ask and then talking for another ten minutes. It's great to be prepared for the questions, but wait for those questions to be asked. Be prepared also not to have all the answers, especially at this early stage. Be honest about what you know, what you don't, and how you may go about finding additional information (usually related to the ask).

Client Success Story

Here's the dynamic with one of our clients. The top leaders, decision-makers, understand innovation is essential to grow the business. The ideas were so unconventional the leaders were uncomfortable. The company hadn't experienced success in the market yet, so there was immense pressure to succeed. The team resourced to bring the new ideas forward were frustrated because they weren't getting any traction, support, or money to advance. They were passionately supporting and championing their projects but going nowhere fast. So, when we were hired, it became clear very quickly that we needed to use a concept we refer to as Flexible Tethering, which offers a bridge from familiar to unfamiliar. "Flexible" because it may need to move or change, and "Tethering" because these are connections but not pillars in concrete.

The team clearly requested what was needed for the project, but the leaders didn't understand the request. They were being asked for something unfamiliar to them and there was no frame of reference. The team had not Flexibly Tethered their request in familiar concepts and behaviors to their company. In their presentation, they had detailed the activities over two phases. We recommended they move from two phases to four phases in their presentation, which allowed for additional granularity on the activities. We also had them add context around what would be learned and what wouldn't be learned. Simple things like the word "prototype" can mean certain things in a company's culture, and this team was using that term quite differently. They also added sections on "next steps if successful." This allowed decision-makers to understand what that next ask might look like.

These slight changes helped the decision-makers' comfort levels increase, and the team was able to get the next level of support needed. Tethering in the familiar was a simple step to take. The projects were able to get the support needed and move forward powerfully.

The ability to sell and influence well is also heavily weighted to the following behaviors: consistent, persistent, non-reactive, actions versus words, and what stage you're in. Remember that Rebel Success is about the unconventional. So when people think about it, it's already outside the norm and not in their warm and fuzzy place.

Consistent

Consistency does two things that are super important to selling and influencing: **It allows others to see your reliability and trustworthiness.** When you call or send a message or have a regular follow-up, you become reliable. Building a relationship with a person has a foundation to grow upon. When you keep your meetings, you're seen as reliable. This earns you the trust of those you would want to work with, sell your product or service to, or want to influence. The second is that it develops behaviors and thought patterns that will become automatic and carry us through the highs and lows. When being consistent is challenging on a good day, just imagine how it is when things are tough. Fortunately, there are electronic tools available today that can help us. Recurring calendar reminders are a popular and easy first step. Customer relationship managers remind us to make contact at a regular frequency. Regular reach outs to our network via social media is best practice.

Most of us have at least one area of our lives in which we are super consistent. This area has become so routine we rarely think about it, and we are usually very good at it. Many of us often have an area of our lives that is lacking consistency. In order to develop consistency in a new area, there are some specific tools we use at Rebel Success for Leaders.

PERSISTENT

Patiently persistent, doggedly persistent. It's the Invincible Rebel characteristic that comes into play. **The ability to keep at it, even when others say it can't be done.** Having a bad day doesn't matter.

A failed test is just information on what doesn't work and what should be adjusted.

Non-reactive

No matter the words they say, the facial expressions they use, or the ghosting (ignoring all communication attempts). Remember, it's tough to be the one with a different idea at a meeting. Being non-reactive means there is no attachment or expectation to the response you're about to get. Rebels tend to be passionate, some would say emotional, about their ideas, and they also tend to be persistent about moving them forward. It can be completely defeating to hear negative feedback, but it can also be incredibly valuable. It's certainly risky in some situations to suggest an unconventional path. Be prepared for the words, facial expressions, and being ignored. So far, my best training ground for this is having a teenager.

The Magic of All In

Are you all in? Or, are you all talk?

When you are selling and influencing your unconventional idea or solutions, the person or group you're talking to can be equally uncomfortable and excited. If what you've said has gotten their attention, they will immediately look at your actions. **Are you**

willing to be the only champion, supporter, proponent, follower? In what ways are your actions lining up with your words? That hot new idea will be dropped faster than a hot potato if your actions aren't backing it up.

I cannot begin to count the number of times that I've personally been all-in, coached my team to be all-in, or worked with consulting clients on the power of all-in. As the champion of the solution, you know the most about it. It's like the person who walks around with a billboard and a microphone. The first few times, people will avoid them or look away. Eventually, you'll read the message and listen to what's said. Over time you'll begin to think about it.

A recent public example is with Greta Thunberg. She's a Swedish environmental activist who has gained international recognition for promoting the view that humanity is facing an existential crisis arising from climate change. She just sat on steps with a sign, regularly. Greta was all-in, and numerous protests and rallies popped up around the world as a result.

In my own experience, if it were myself or my team who was developing and promoting a new idea, we talked about it to everyone, brought it up in conversations, sought input on how to improve, and looked for support to advance it. The two biggest examples from my experience went on to commercial viability with large price tags attached to them. The time frame for these things can be long—multi-year—but if I wasn't all-in and other leaders weren't also all-in, nothing would have happened. The idea, the potential, and the ultimate successes would have evaporated.

There's a need to substantiate your idea or solution. This is something you can plan for, design a project around, and make progress against. There's also a proof period that's difficult to plan for. It's when people watch for your behaviors and signals. How consistent are you? Do you switch off from one idea to another when you don't get support? Or do you stick with it and constantly seek ways to improve?

When you've passed the proof period, people see you're all-in.

STAGES

Achieving Rebel Success includes a basic awareness of the stages of the process. These can be different depending on category, industry, or nonprofit. Give some thought to the breakdown that seems to make sense. Start with only four stages. Use your own labels.

General examples of the four areas may include:

- development, prototype, testing, scale product

- research, evaluation, technology validation, viability assessment

- stakeholder or user feedback, ideation of solution, development of priority solution, feedback or fit testing.

What's the main activity in each area, and what are the one to three supporting activities?

REBEL TALENTS

We've all be around those people who just seem to have that something extra. Most of the time, it's hard to put your finger on what it is, but you know it's something. In my experience, there are a couple of areas where Rebels seem to have unique characteristics that only aid in helping them be successful. Some organizations would call these soft skills, and the actions are very individualized. Everyone starts in a different place. We'll review them at a high level here.

The first is magnetism. There's a section in this book called "Upping Your Rebel Magnetism." Those people with personas that just seem to attract what they need are definitely more successful. The question is, how can a person do more of this?

The second is translation. Unconventional ideas are hard to understand and grasp. Sometimes Rebels just see things that others don't. Rebels can be successful faster if they can bring their idea to life to others. Similar to the section in this book on "Translating the Unconventional," it's about how to translate it to something that's simple and reproducible. This makes adoption easier and speed to support a lot faster.

The third is to embrace opposition. Even crave it! These people seem undaunted by the opposition. They're not oblivious and refusing to take constructive feedback, but not defeated or set back by it. Seek the opposition and enjoy getting the opposing points of view and hearing the concerns.

The fourth is to gain expertise in conventional success measures. The ability to sell and influence to Rebel Success can be accelerated when you know the elements of success that conventional ideas go through.

When working with clients on this fourth talent, their instinct is typically to use the same person that's been heavily involved at the beginning of the process and develop their skills on this talent with the same project. We advise against that approach and instead recommend that the experience is gained on a different project. Below are some of the strategies we've used in different situations.

Larger companies have the ability to move their talent around the organization to gain experience. With a deliberate placement strategy, short- and long-term assignments can be very valuable strategies to achieve the fourth talent. Deliberately resourcing two individuals with different skills to work closely on a project is effective when you are able to match openness, interest, and can clearly define deliverables so that cross experiences can be gained.

Training can be utilized and is effective when there's a project that can be immediately used to apply learnings.

Ensuring support for the person you've identified as talented and you've tapped to gain this new experience is critical. Their environment will change dramatically in this new role, and they will be obvious and unconventional in the sea of similarity you've just placed them. Set them up to thrive.

CHAPTER FIFTEEN

NOTHING BUT UPSIDE

The offices were really trendy and bright with great furniture, and all of the agency folks were dressed like they could have been in a fashion magazine sporting the funkiest glasses I'd ever seen. I woke up excited to go to this meeting. I was selected to be part of a great team for a new innovative platform, and we were kicking off the project in New York. We'd started in a conference room when a late arrival came in, saying, "Something happened to the World Trade Center." After a couple of stops and starts, we all realized this was real, and it was serious. The meeting was canceled.

It dawned on me: I was really close, not Ground Zero, but at 26th Street. I was in an unfamiliar city with communication temporarily cut off outside Manhattan. Two streams of thoughts ran through my head simultaneously. Rational: staying calm, problem-solving planning contingencies, checking what I had brought in my luggage, trying to call home. Irrational: *Is this an attack? Are we in danger? How will we get home? Will I get home?*

Stepping outside for the first time, the skyscrapers were eerie. It was a bright sunny day with a cool breeze. Sun glistened off the water features between the buildings. It was completely silent in New York City.

No cars were moving on the road. People who were out on the street whispered to each other and huddled in groups. Walking to the corner, black smoke was visible through the buildings, but it just looked like a fire. The towers hadn't fallen yet. I spotted one person in a business suit, covered in ash, walking alone in the middle of the street from the direction of the smoke—face black, hair sooty, one shoe missing. Shell-shocked described the look on his face. Someone stopped to speak to him and asked if he needed help. He shook his head and just kept walking in the same direction toward Midtown. Would there be more? Why was he the only person we saw?

Back inside, I regrouped, took care of the necessities, and finally called loved ones. I had only been married a little over a year, and my husband was panicked, my parents even worse. The next stop was Union Station in Midtown. If you've ever been to NYC, you'll know it's never quiet, not even at night. The walk was without traffic, none. No horns honking, no people yelling at each other. I hardly passed any people. It was as if time stood still. All exits to Manhattan were blocked to traffic. The underground news within Manhattan said the trains were running outbound only.

There were two options. If we made it to an exit off Manhattan (pretty long walk) through corporate connections, we could be connected with drivers who were stationed to help us. The alternative was taking the train out to a corporate satellite office and potentially finding a rental car. The minute you walked into the train station, it was like walking into another extreme. It was teaming with people running between urgency and panic, a lot of yelling and pointing directions. Staff pushed us through turnstiles. "Don't pay, just get on a train and get out." Emotionally exhausted passengers were packed into trains and sent off. Nerves were frayed to the edge and sometimes past the breaking point. The staff did their best, and passengers tried to help each other, but the skepticism was now strongly rooted. No one knew if this was the end of what was planned for the day. It was a leap of faith to get on the train. What if this was a bad idea and we'd all die in an explosion underground?

All rental cars in the area were cut off, and all flights nationwide were grounded. People stepped up. They seemed to need a connection and reminder of positive humanity in the wake of unspeakable terror. We made a connection with someone who let us sleep on her floor and drove us far enough into New Jersey the next morning to get a car. It was a very long drive home to Chicago. The roads were empty for most of the 790 miles. Stopping meant sharing stories among the few travelers in the rest areas. The comradery of support from strangers was as strong as the hunger for information.

Each mile we drove represented coming out of something profoundly horrible and moving toward something optimistic and hopeful. The gift was to take the next step. There's only an upside.

September 11 was a profound experience for many. It instilled in me a grounding of priorities in life, a reminder of my sense of purpose and that, no matter what, there's always another step to take. Through the market crash of 2008 and the global pandemic of 2020, there was always another step to be taken, a purpose to be working toward. What do Rebel Leaders do amidst profound experiences and changes outside our control?

Once the initial reaction and immediate assessment are over, the next steps are:

Reflection. Take stock of your situation and include the personal and professional aspects as well as past and future. Are you where you want to be? There's almost always a gap somewhere that needs to be heard, tended to, filled, developed.

Shed the bricks. Get rid of that stuff you don't need or want to carry any longer. You may have been intentionally carrying the burden for your team. You may not have realized how many bricks there actually were. These bricks may have once been pebbles, and now they are too big to carry. They are familiar, but you can let them go.

Deliberate steps of intention. Rebel Leaders always move toward something. It might be into discovery, exploration, or action in a certain direction. But, the steps are always deliberate, and there's always an upside.

Resilience. That's what you see with the Rebel Leader.

LEVEL UP*

- Where could you spend some time? Is it in reflection or shedding some bricks you already are tired of carrying?

- If you're stuck on the deliberate steps of intention, find someone you know, like, and trust to help you through the process.

---

* All Level Up activities can be found in the Appendix

PART THREE

UNLEASH THE REVOLUTION OF INNOVATION

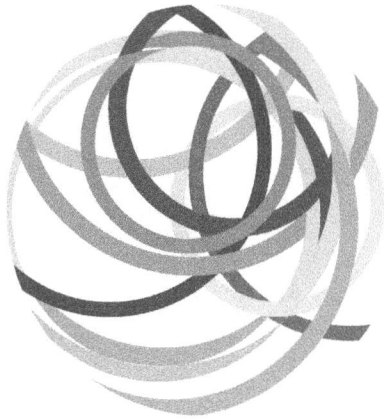

CHAPTER SIXTEEN

UNSTOPPABLE

Once an individual can be heard, they will share unconventional ideas freely. When a team is transparent with each other, all of the talents of the team can be utilized fully. A person who is fully heard will stick around because of the value they add. A team will stay together because they are doing what's right versus what the leader wants to hear. Solution-minded teams are fully engaged and operate with speed and rigor. When teams are transparent, they are more effective and solve problems faster, and projects get done quickly and accurately. When someone is heard, and the team is transparent, a team is allowed to create freely.

Rebel Success environments get results fast. Once you've established a Rebel Success Environment, the revolution of innovation is unleashed. This section of the book will cover ways to guide and shape that Rebel Success environment over time.

Let's revisit the Rebel Rating characteristics for reference. We use these in many ways with our consulting clients. They can be used to not only describe individuals and identify development gaps but characterize parts of organizations. We also use them to work with leaders to develop themselves and their teams across career evolution. As you review this list, how are you tapping into all of these Rebel Characteristics to move your goals and vision forward as a leader and for your organization?

- **Innovator**: Highly creative thinkers (conceptualize) and doers (bring concepts to life); tends to become immersed in a seemingly impossible situation; with time and thorough assessment are able to see a vision of an elegant and simple solution; a new future state.

- **Explorer**: Loves discovery and learning; seeks a range of inputs to form opinions and direction, including those seemingly contrary, or against, their own; seemingly wired and comfortable going against conventional beliefs or norms; some see this as fearless.

- **Invincible**: Rises to the challenge when others don't believe in them; comfortable digging into the details to find solutions; in fact, when told something can't be done, that excites them and adds fuel to their motivation; persistent; determined; disciplined.

- **Influencer**: Highly tuned relationship and communication skills to influence others for support; able to articulate the value of an idea versus just the technical details; they maintain and leverage their network and are connected to other networks; very savvy with conventional requirements of success and can use that advantageously for unconventional ideas.

If you are ready to take things to the next level, we have a special offer at the end of the book. Make sure to check it out to learn more.

CHAPTER SEVENTEEN

ALIGN, ACTIVATE, CULTIVATE

You can use the Rebel index to determine where you are as a leader and where your team, organization, or group is. That's your starting point. Now, how do you foster those Rebel Leader characteristics in yourself and your team?

ALIGN

The assessment should give you a baseline. Not every person needs or wants to be good at all characteristics. If where you want to be in life or in your professional pursuits needs to change, then the Rebel Rating should guide you to the areas of concentration and focus. After completing the assessment, choose a characteristic you are already strong in and perhaps one that you would like to strengthen. If there are multiple areas to focus on, choose one to start with.

The best success rate is when goals are connected to the area you want to work on. **Alignment gives you the opportunity to demonstrate new skill development and to see increased success as a result.**

Lisa wanted to influence more decision-makers to her new product ideas. She had great success creating the ideas but often wasn't able to garner support. After taking the assessment, she decided it was time to become better at influencing others, selling her idea so that it could get developed. She could have just gotten information and not acted on it, but Lisa decided it was time for a change. We worked together on her goals and new behaviors so that she had opportunities to demonstrate the new ways of influencing others with her ideas. She was super successful and ended up getting close to one of the business partners and ultimately advanced her career through promotion. My leadership was thrilled with the increased performance of my group.

You'll need a structured relationship to maintain progress and accountability along the way. It's most often a business objective that you're working on with a manager, mentor, or a team. Or if there isn't a natural structure to hold you accountable, invest in a coach that will help you progress. Often the decision to invest is enough to hold you accountable. You can never go wrong with a decision to improve yourself.

Alignment requires choice. Decision. Clarity. If those steps haven't been taken, an alignment will feel elusive. Just do it!

ACTIVATE THE REBEL'S INNER POWER

Activation is like putting your foot on the gas in a car. Once you activate, your destinations are endless. These new ways of approaching problems may feel very uncomfortable, and people tend not to take risks, especially when they aren't very good at something. There is a set of mental directions we give ourselves: Head Talk. Most people have thoughts that are random and race wildly from one topic to another. They are at the mercy of emotion and habit.

> *"Does your mind have control over you, or are*
> *you going to have control of your mind?"*
> —*Olympic silver medalist Galen Rupp*

Instead, what are the behaviors, routines, and rituals that strengthen and direct your mind via your Head Talk? Let's take sales as an example since so many people seem to have a dislike for it and the people who do it. Everyone sells something—products, services, ideas, opinions. Kids learn at an early age to sell (or influence) parents on sleepovers, staying out late, purchases of expensive electronics, or the need for specific clothes. **There are three critical steps to take in strengthening your mind and the quality of your Head Talk:**

1. Imagine it

2. Write it down

3. Speak it

Imagine how it will feel to be successful. What will people you know say, what will you feel like, will it be a sunny day, will you be in your car? It may sound odd at first, but create in your mind the snapshot of the event of success. Make sure you imagine yourself enjoying it! That's super important since you're probably starting out with apprehension or fear, not knowing what to do with this new skill. Don't worry at first about what you'll say to sell this thing, but imagine what the other person will say. Imagine how they will experience the value of what you have to offer.

Write it down. There's a connection our brain makes when we move from visualizing something to writing it down. It's a way of saying you're serious. You can start with bullet points, then move to sentences. Again, be descriptive and use the elements of what you've imagined. Most people at this stage will begin to form goals: one overarching goal with the smaller goals (steps) it will take to accomplish it. You may even create SMART goals: specific, measurable, achievable, relevant, time-bound. Write down what you are going to sell and how you will address all the objections. What are all the different ways your idea, product, or service provides value? Write down what the other person will say, and your friends and family will say when they hear about it.

Speak it. Say it out loud and repeat it. Be very descriptive. The easiest way to start is to speak what you've written, which is what you've imagined. Speak it to a trusted friend. Talk to your mentors, your spouse, or significant other. Ultimately you should be talking to people who are in a position to make this happen with you. Perhaps it's a well-networked friend who is able to introduce you to someone in the field. Maybe it's a social connection you can ask to share time over coffee whose business is in an area you may market and sell your product or service.

Success Story:

John had been working on a particular idea for a new product for years but had not been successful in selling it to the stakeholders. When he and I started working together, he was really negative about his chances for success. He'd tried so many times in the past and had failed. He seemed to have the fundamentals down but was talking himself out of success.

So we started by having him tell me about the meeting: who will attend, what will they say, and what information they'll require from the presentation. I asked what would need to happen for it to be successful. How would he feel in a successful meeting?

I asked him to write down each question he had already heard, the ones he still anticipates and the answers he'd provide. We worked on ensuring his written responses were clear, succinct, and value-based. Then we rehearsed his answers. I, of course, threw in some new ones to help him gain the confidence he could handle those. His next opportunity to sell his idea was very successful!

Now that you've addressed Head Talk, there's still the work. After all, the mind can't take the place of actually doing the work. There are many ways to get started. Plans can be designed for individuals and for teams that can be as detailed as desired, along with monitoring and assessment steps.

The simplest starting point is to choose one characteristic or trait. Be intentional about your commitment to this area. Create a daily behavior to advance your abilities. Choose only one at a time and continue it for three months. Read books on the topic. Build your network of people in the area in which you want to be better. This might mean reaching out to those already in your network but talking about a different area of interest. Attend networking events and build connections around those areas of interest.

CULTIVATE YOUR INNER POWER

"Don't be afraid to do what you don't think you can."
—Andy Drennan, Senior VP,
Food Processing Suppliers Association

I love this quote. Stop being limited by our thoughts, and instead be open to truly discovering capabilities. Be open to doing far more than we ever thought possible.

If you've put into action any of the suggestions up to this point, you'll likely feel both liberated and terrified. Liberated because those beliefs, ideas, or passions are getting their deserved airtime. Terrified because these skills are little more than infants, needing constant attention and support. Without this high level of care, they may not grow and reach their full potential. Have a specific plan to continue to grow. Many people use mornings to have accountability and routine for themselves. It's often helpful to have an accountability partner or coach to provide guidance and support.

Personally, I've used a variety of tools to put new behaviors into practice. What I've found is that there isn't one practice that works for every behavior. The common theme in all of them is to be deliberate and daily. Below are examples of tools and how I've used them.

Tools you can use to bring new behaviors forward:

- **Sales process**: Daily accountability texts to the accountability partner

- **Focus on development with my team**: Thirty minute block before each one on one, where I review their plan and formulate my questions before the meeting

- **Be accessible to my team**: Block no meeting time on my calendar

- **Affirmations**: Written in the morning or a calendar reminder that has them written in the reminder

- **Goal visualization**: For this book, I'd visualize it finished, holding it, signing it, speaking about its topics

What about your team, your group? How do you start or continue to cultivate Rebel Success in them? To cultivate is to prepare, work on, develop, and improve. Setting an example as a leader is often a way to raise the bar on expectations. What you do is what you expect them to do, regardless of saying otherwise. So, if you are demonstrating or modeling the behavior, they will get that. What you reward gets seen and sets an expectation on what you value. Look at the rewards and acknowledgment you have in place or perhaps just verbally communicate. Those are the actions your team begins to understand as expectations. Look at how you set up their roles and their goals.

I think the most challenging shift was getting out of the mindset that people with experience should actually just make all the decisions. Especially in a startup environment, if you know the answer, it's really convenient to go with that and let people rely upon you. Then you never develop other domain expertise. How do you remove yourself from doing that default of just providing the answer in a meeting? It's really easy to fall into that trap and become a crutch. In my career, I personally had embraced learning from mistakes, but then I would answer questions for people. What I really learned is you have to give people the freedom. If you really want someone to be bought into your organization, it's important to allow them to learn and make those mistakes. They should go through the process to figure it out without others jumping in and solving the problem or saving the day for them every time. That's an incredibly difficult mind shift, and it requires a significant amount of willingness to become self-aware and to practice my mindfulness.

—James Stephens, CEO, *Blue Marble Biomaterials*

CHAPTER EIGHTEEN

THE SUSTAINED ADVANTAGE

"One person can be a change catalyst, a 'transformer'
in any situation, any organization. Such an individual
is yeast that can leaven an entire loaf. It requires
vision, initiative, patience, respect, persistence,
courage, and faith to be a transforming leader."
—Steven Covey

The energy of activation is greater than the energy required to maintain the status quo. It is possible to adjust the reaction and energy required by addition of a catalyst. Adding a bit more yeast to the recipe can sometimes reduce the speed to leaven. Bakers may also add vitamin C to speed the gluten development. With a catalyst, the entire loaf can operate at a new level. That momentum can be relied on for some time to be the new normal. Once the individual or team is at the new level, the idea is to stay with momentum as long as possible. Ride the wave. This is the time strategically where you maintain market position. Naturally, because of the momentum, your team often solves problems before you're aware of them.

With appropriate strategies, this is the time to impact the most people with your offering.

Sustaining your advantage doesn't mean riding the high forever. There will always be a dip, or a phase when this momentum is reduced. Acknowledging this and instead of trying to avoid it, plan for your reaction. It doesn't mean to avoid it or go around it or push through it. A disciplined process and approach to the low spots means not only are they are expected, but they are often shorter and less intense. Overall the business impact in the short term is lessened. Over the long term, they are manageable instead of surprising. Once you expect and plan for the dips, they can be strategically leveraged for steady increases.

Success Story:

I had a client who was experiencing this sustained higher level of momentum. She and the team were enjoying every minute of the successes and recognition they were getting. People were eagerly coming in early and working longer hours because they were energized about the success they were experiencing. She was very shocked and upset one day when I asked for her future plan when her team would naturally experience the dip, or drop off, in momentum.

Her perspective was that her team was performing well and she was overjoyed that they had achieved this high level of performance. Never before in her career had she figured this out. She felt this should be the new normal, so it shouldn't need to stop or change. Many leaders feel this way because it's exciting and they are often reaching new heights and career successes. They are often blinded by the success and are unable to see that the success leads to a new starting point for themselves and their teams. Eventually, it became clear to her that her team would naturally transition this work and need to start the process of getting the next project going.

We had enough time to begin to transition her team through a recovery period. People scheduled vacations and time with family. She was able to send two members of the team to critical development and technical meetings that are difficult to schedule. When the dip came, her team was better positioned to expect it.

RECOVERY

People and systems need time for recovery. During significant phases of exponential business, growth maintenance, and efficiency tasks fall by the side. People are working long hours, and over time. Fatigue will increase. The energy at full throttle is drained over time. People are the biggest asset of any organization, and they need to recover and begin to think about the next idea and business challenges. Business systems need to be reset and perhaps remodeled to ensure the support structure for your market offering is seamlessly presented and delivered. In many areas, second chances don't happen.

As an individual, take the time to reset your healthy habits. Exponential growth phases equate to your body operating consistently in fight-or-flight mode. Reset to recovery mode. Read something new. Expose yourself to a new hobby or area of the competitive market. This gives your mind the much-needed space to grow and be curious in new areas. Gathering inputs for your next idea is another great place to focus energies.

Phasing

If your portfolio or organization is large enough, it will be important to plan such that projects are in different phases at any given time. This allows the leader to look across the portfolio and switch gears between projects as appropriate. The project team also has the time to shift gears to the next focus area. This strategy allows the overall business to experience more consistency versus widely changing peaks and valleys. If you are strategically using a separate team, that's best for the focus and energy of the team.

As a leader, do not skip your individual recovery phase. You are uniquely watched by the organization and need to maintain the energy to focus at a high level. The other timing aspect to consider is that your personal growth cycles should follow a different curve to that of the teams.

Growth and Rejuvenation

Ultimately when talent remains static, the business will decline. Development of yourself and the team is a priority. To a certain degree, this can happen during periods of growth if team members are demonstrating new skills and growing through doing. There is also much growth that can happen during recovery phases. It's very easy to get caught up in the demands of the immediate business concerns and skip over the rejuvenation period.

When working with individual leaders, we often talk about two main areas: the first is if they are taking their vacation time and how to plan that out, and the second is how they get an amount of time every day for themselves. Vacation time tends to be taken if it's scheduled, paid for, and communicated out to the team. The daily time can be a bit more challenging, as it needs to be protected from demands from many different directions.

Suzanne and I worked together to figure out how to get daily time to herself. What seemed to work best was morning time. She'd get the family going at home and drive to the same coffee house, set a timer for thirty minutes, and then continue to the office. For her, she needed time away from both home and office to really focus on herself. In the beginning, she had a list of options I gave her to work on at that time: reading, journaling, podcasts. Eventually, she evolved and occasionally used this time to work on the vision for her team. Her feedback to me was that this helped her be present for her team, focus her priorities, and limit distractions.

CHAPTER NINETEEN

START THE REVOLUTION

Why even consider a revolution of innovation? Once the behaviors and characteristics are set, it just happens. Ideas flow, inputs are heard, and teams operate with transparency and at a high level of efficiency. The job of the leader becomes steering the ship versus fixing the engine room and plugging the holes.

Everyone wants to have a great new idea that offers valuable change. You'll know when you've started the revolution when all sorts of other people start to speak, write, and blog about it as if it's their idea. They take the idea nugget and make it their own with slight differences and adaptations. They've built upon what started and made it more useful. Lots of companies are making money on different styles and types of smartphones, but the first one was revolutionary.

The desired endpoint, the big audacious goal, is an innovation that changes behaviors and is sustained over periods of time, whether that's market share for your business, empowering youth in your community, or being the movement of change for social injustice. Think and act in a big way! Start the revolution of innovation from within your team, organization, company, and even your personal passions outside of work. People need to bring ideas, solutions, and innovations that, in some way, affect them personally or professionally. Almost never is anyone in a position to throw a business out when it's not working. That would be like throwing the baby out with the bath water. You can't stop social services when the system is broken.

"If you want to rebel, rebel from inside the system. That's much more powerful than rebelling outside the system."
—Marie Lu

The business community has successfully started innovation outside the core, but the assimilation back to the mothership is woefully unsuccessful. Acquiring companies and operating as separate entities can be great for balance sheets for a period of time, but it never solves the problem with the core mothership that continues to suffer. Thinking you can fix someone else's problem will not succeed without the support and buy-in from the people living it every day. **Influence from within. People understand why the change is coming because you are living it also. Start a revolution of innovation from within. The end result will be much more powerful and exciting.**

CLIENT STORY

I had a great opportunity to work with a company to assist with how they leveraged innovation from another company. The first meeting included teams from both organizations plus myself. The objective was to share innovation platforms and strategies to determine how everyone can work together. The company I was working with presented the select ideas of the other company that had innovation potential and the strategy of where we could go together. There was oddly little discussion or collaboration on building those ideas together but the ideas were solid, creative, and unconventional.

The team I walked in with had not involved anyone at the company we visited in the development of the ideas or the presentation. It was a completely one-sided perspective! That specific joint collaboration opportunity did not go anywhere. I felt like the team missed out on truly understanding the client (the other company) and actually hearing their needs and thoughts. This step was skipped, and an opportunity to collaborate with the client (the other company) was missed. We have to remember to involve everyone in the process of creation. It's critical to truly understand the issue that needs to be resolved and involving those that have a stake in the resolution process.

Starting a revolution of innovation relies heavily on the skills of the Invincibles and the Influencers. It's all about the *why* of the change. Determination and persistence are going to be critical to overcome the eventual obstacles. The ability to craft communication that clearly paints a picture of the *why* and inspires others to action will influence others in the required support. There is a deliberate switch in focus from the *what* to the *value* and the *why*.

Building a network of supporters in advance is also critical to success. Robert Cialdini from Arizona State University describes the six sources of influence in his book, *Influence*, as:

1. Likability

2. Reciprocity

3. Social proof: do others buy-in?

4. Consistency: doing what you say

5. Scarcity of resources: the value of what's scarce

6. Authority: are you an expert?

Review what was covered in the "Selling Fearlessly" and the "Align, Activate, Cultivate" sections to build your message. Determine the biggest objections to be well prepared as you sell your ideas. Remember: there's work to be done before the revolution part.

When you're ready, there are three points to focus on when starting the revolution of innovation. Your efforts need to be simple, sharable, and top of mind. Doing these things will position you to go viral with your idea or solution.

THREE POINTS TO FOCUS ON:

Simple: The idea needs to be communicated simply. How many different people with different skills and backgrounds can understand and repeat the idea or solution?

Sharable: Before the popularity of social media, shareability meant that someone else needed to be knowledgeable and share your idea independently of you in the conversation. Now with social media prevalence, it's especially important that you share out your idea, solution, or content. Getting your message out there is easier than ever before and it's more powerful to connect authentically.

Top of mind: Within your networks, this means that they know you and what you are about in your business. When they meet others, you and your solution pop into their minds. They make connections for you, on your behalf, seamlessly. Ignoring your network is a mistake and synonymous with missed potential and opportunity. A healthy and consistent networking behavior is critical for success.

"We guide leaders to embrace their own individual diverse and inclusive perspective and to take action on behalf of that. This begets innovation."

—Sarah Alter, President and CEO, Network of Executive Women

CHAPTER TWENTY

OWN THE GAP

Unleashing a revolution needs a leader or multiple leaders. Sometimes, those are obvious; other times, not. All of those leaders on their revolution journey grew exponentially. They had convictions and ideas and were able to garner followers. They also owned their personal development and what they needed to work on to achieve the objective.

Whether you think you can or think you can't, you're right. Unleashing the revolution of innovation requires agile learners. There is always something new to learn, a new level to reach, and a new experience that can deepen your understanding. **A gap is an opportunity and offers a new and exciting understanding once you've closed that gap.**

The deliberate, intentional movement toward an end goal will close the gap. This is about *you*, Mr. or Ms. Leader. Back to the law of attraction, you attract what you are, whether it's positive or negative, high or low energy, rebellious people or status quo people, successful or unsuccessful. **Know your gaps. Own them. Work tirelessly to close them. And then move on to the next one.**

REBEL SUCCESS FOR LEADERS

Peter Drucker recommended following effective action with quiet reflection. This is about absorbing the action and learning from it.

> *"If you don't take a step back and pause from what you thought was the career goal, evaluate what you learned, how your growing and adapting, you may be actually limiting yourself. The destination may have shifted."*
>
> —*Jennifer Wulf, Director of Sales, Graphic Packaging International*

Cultivate self-awareness and deepen self-understanding. This is equally about what you do as well as why you do it. What are your motivations?

There's no complicated science here, but it can often be very challenging to self-assess gaps and address them. These assessments call into question confidence, self-worth, values, and fears of success. **The most successful people in the world work with a coach to become better versions of themselves. Find someone you know, like, and trust and who can help you own the gap between where you are and where you want to be.** Use the relationship with a coach to help you embrace complexity and begin to tackle each aspect of new growth, one at a time.

CHAPTER TWENTY-ONE

EVOLVE YOUR REBEL TALENT

It's not a sprint; it's a marathon. Not the destination, but the journey.

As you work to put in place behaviors that will cultivate your Rebel talent and create a revolution of innovation, you will create success and affect change. As with all new skills and behaviors, the more they're used, the more proficient you become at them. **The speed of information and change is accelerating. Those individuals who are able to pivot and work well within that environment will be successful.** How does your team respond to the speed of change, and how can you help them evolve their skills?

Experiences working in an emergency room were very useful to draw on in my business career. Triage, or the process of ranking patients by severity of need, could be very fast-paced and driven by one emergency after another, with no way to control what came through the door. It's about quickly getting the screening information needed and making the first-pass decision about severity. Not every patient is treated in a linear fashion before the next patient. Neither is every business challenge.

Circumstances will evolve, and new challenges will arise. Look for those inflection points, where, either internally or externally, things have shifted. One day, the team will be working hard on how to influence others to your ideas, and the next, they'll be exploring new paths. **Be prepared to evolve with the situation or be prepared to change your circumstances.** Have a strategy for who on the team is particularly strong at certain skills because you want to have individuals work to their strengths. Always make sure you have double coverage for each skill. Evolve aptitude for a skill into expertise for a skill. This will not only help avoid burnout but will improve job satisfaction as you invest in the growth of your team.

Career evolution is a common topic in this area. It's very important to garner experiences that grow your talents in areas of strengths as well as those areas adjacent to strengths. I use the adjacent term to refer to areas where an individual may have the aptitude or may be undeveloped, driven by a lack of experience. Creating new skills from a set of circumstances you've either been handed or have freely walked to on your own is a significant transition skill to master. Evolving talent to master the transitions will accelerate success. **New always takes longer, but the faster it can be mastered, the faster you can move.**

Strong Rebel talent can serve you well. Work through the four areas in the Rebel Rating to create the path to what's next. Get a coach to help you or your team through the process; it can go a lot faster and can be more pleasant.

CHAPTER TWENTY-TWO

INVEST IN YOUR REBEL TALENT

"You don't want to hear about the projects? The details of where everything is and what I'm doing."

I reply to my team member, "Do you need me to help with an introduction, break down a barrier, or to free up resources? Are you telling me you're behind on deliverables?"

"Well, no, everything is on track. I thought you needed the details."

I reply, "What I'd love to spend our time on is your approach to communicate clearly, and with confidence, the team's innovations. The last presentation didn't go as you wanted. You've been working on some adjustments to that communication, and I'm available to review and offer feedback. I can share my thoughts on what each of the folks in the room may ask so that you are prepared in advance."

This conversation was repeated with every team member for a couple of months. They were so used to leaders who needed the details that they almost didn't know how to respond when our conversations centered on the development of their skills and competencies. One year, I decided to focus on the development of my team. It was super risky because all the leaders around me were focusing on the details of the projects, but it was super successful!

Leaders are measured on the performance of their team against goals. But people love it when others invest in them. Mentor, coach, develop them into better versions of themselves. The Millennial group has been labeled negatively for demanding development at companies they work for. Who in their right mind doesn't want their company to invest in them? It seems to me as though that culture shift was needed. We won't remember who measured our goals, but we will remember those mentors, coaches, and teachers who invested in us.

> *"Find a culture that is willing to take bets on you,*
> *and that will give you a nice long and wide runway.*
> *They will embrace that inner rebel in you."*
> —Sarah Alter, President and CEO, Network of Executive Women

What you invest in does need to be strategically connected with the demonstration of goals. It's not about micromanaging time or attending meetings with the team. How have you left that person, that individual, in a better place, with more career opportunities, exposure to influential people, promotion, a new role, the ability to follow a passion, or increased self-confidence? **We, at Rebel**

Success for Leaders, work with companies and teams to better invest in their talent for success.

CHAPTER TWENTY-THREE

LIVE IT NOW!

It was volunteer day—a day of giving back. The day I met Bill.

It was an ugly warehouse building that had been converted into transitional housing for men who had been released from prison. The building was divided into living quarters, donated clothing, common areas, and staff space. The purpose was to acclimate them to life outside and give them key skills and clothes to start over. These men had no one else, no family or friends, to help them through it.

My assignment for the day was to help with interviewing skills. A group of these men would soon be moving into that phase of their stay. They were supported through a period of time to find work and then ultimately move out into more permanent housing. My coworker, a guy, pulled together a plan to meet these men and talk to them a bit. Then, we'd schedule mock interviews, so they had a chance to practice.

I walked over to two chairs set in an area in the middle of the floor with a small table in the middle. Bill swallowed up this chair. He barely fit. He was huge. As I walked over, he went from hunched over to slowly unwinding each limb of his body. As he stood up, he towered over me at 6'5", with tattoos on most of his exposed arms and some of his face and neck. One scar went from his forehead to under his ear. I could see he'd kept busy with the weights in prison, I imagine as a way to pass the time and protect himself. He quickly glanced at me but didn't hold eye contact.

By this point, I was a bit unsettled but still determined to contribute. I introduced myself and asked his name. "Bill," he said. Bill and the others had heard why we were there from the staff, but I explained our purpose again. As it turned out, Bill had already had a couple of interviews, and I asked him how they went.

This huge man, who could probably pick me up with one finger, just crumpled. He slumped over and looked defeated.

"Just bad," he said.

"Why was it bad?" I asked.

This is when he looked up and made eye contact with me. "Little lady, don't you know you have to tell them you're a convicted felon?"

The first thought I had was, *that question is on every application.* And the second thought was, *I'm sitting here with a convicted felon!* I did a good job controlling my nerves, as his seemed worse than mine.

When I asked what he usually says to that question, "Not much" was the answer.

"I'm not used to talking to women and them being in that chair. Women didn't use to do that stuff."

I said, "Bill, you obviously can't lie about it. That would make things worse. Is there anything you can tell me about how you got to prison and what you want to do with your life now? We'll work on talking to women in the interview practice."

From a young age, Bill grew up in a gang. It was his community, as well as his way of survival. The protection offered kept him alive, but there were things he was required to do for this protection. More than twenty-five years prior, Bill and one of the other gang members robbed a gas station. In the heat of the moment, the owner was shot, and Bill was the one who was found at the scene.

"Look, I'm not proud of what happened. I didn't pull the trigger, but I was there. Now, my life is over because if it."

Bill had served his time and was now looking to start over.

"What do you hope to do now that you're out?"

"I've seen a lot inside and had a lot of regrets. I want a job, and I want a chance to be an honorable man. This place here is a good place. They help people like me. Maybe I'll help others too. Not everyone had a fair shot at life."

"Well, Bill, let's get you ready to have your fair shot in life."

He dressed up well and was pretty presentable in an interview suit. My coworker and I gave Bill and the others interview practice with both of us. Beyond practicing answers to the most common interview questions, we really had them focus on how they wanted to contribute in the future, the type of work they would do, why they would be a good employee.

As we were wrapping up for the day, Bill came over, stood very solemnly in front of me, with a tear rolling down his face.

"Little lady—I'm sorry. I'm not supposed to call you that. Thank you for coming today and for helping the rest of us guys and me. It's been a long time since someone believed in me."

We left that day feeling like we'd invested in the lives of those men and made a true difference. I kept in touch with the staff at the center and eventually learned that Bill had made it to the next stage, a stable job, and he moved on. That lesson has stayed with me.

Believe in what people can become. Show them how and walk with them along the way.

Take the leap; be the Rebel!

REBEL SUCCESS FOR LEADERS

We all have an inner Rebel. The quotes of leaders from various industries in this book show that Rebel success can happen everywhere. The personal stories and examples show that it's not just a business concept. This is very relevant to your personal lives and ambitions as well.

Rebel Success is about knowing how to use your passions and strengths in a very deliberate and focused way. It all starts with enabling your inner Rebel and identifying your Rebel Why. Next is using the techniques, processes, and steps to grow and nurture your game-changing ideas to succeed.

There are no limits! Just deliberate, fearless steps to take. Just start.

BONUS

EXCLUSIVE INVITATION

If you do everything in this book, especially the Level Up sections, you'll see a dramatic change, shift, and improvement.

But why stop there?

Join our group of clients and take the Rebel Rating. You'll get a next-level insight into which of the Rebel Characteristics are strengths and which you could strategically improve.

Then, you have a consultation with me—that's right, it's actually me—to review your results and how they match up with your goals.

https://rebelsuccessforleaders.com/book-RebelRating/

LEVEL UP ACTIVITIES

LEVEL UP ACTIVITY 1 FROM CHAPTER 8

Think of the people you know and those who seem to have strong Rebel Characteristics. Describe someone you think is a Rebel and then use that example to consider how you can grow to a new level of success personally.

- List three traits you admire in that person

- List three traits you believe you personally have

- List three traits you would like to become better at

LEVEL UP ACTIVITY 2 FROM CHAPTER 8

Depending on where you are, focus on one main area and list two potential things you, as the leader, could do differently to support the change that is needed.

- Two criteria to add to a new team member search

- Two elements to consider adding to an onboarding process

- Two actions you can take to set the stage for the upcoming change.

LEVEL UP ACTIVITY 3 FROM CHAPTER 8

- Using the four Rebel traits of innovator, explorer, invincible, influencer, consider two current team members and what might they do differently.

- Where might they have underdeveloped potential? Where might you provide stretch opportunities?

- What are the ways you'll have the conversation with them about the potential you see and how you'd like to encourage it?

LEVEL UP ACTIVITY 1 FROM CHAPTER 9

Consider a successful team you've been a part of or led.

- What were the key components of success for that team?

- Were there best practices you learned in that experience and continue to use?

LEVEL UP ACTIVITY 2 FROM CHAPTER 9

Determine one to three ideas that you personally as a leader, would like to explore using a new and different approach in the following three areas:

1. Ideas for the organization

2. Ideas for the team

3. Ideas for yourself

LEVEL UP ACTIVITY FROM CHAPTER 10

Choose two Rebel behaviors you could model to someone else to advance their skills or development.

- How will you be available to provide feedback as they demonstrate their approach the first time?

- What are the important elements between the two approaches that should be consistent, and what are those elements where there's freedom to change?

LEVEL UP ACTIVITY FROM CHAPTER 11

Below are four questions to get you started. As you consider each question, assess where you are versus where you want to be. Describe the circumstances in detail. What you say, how you feel, what are other people's perspectives of you, what are your thoughts and expectations?

How would you describe your answers to these four questions today?

- Do you enjoy working in the unknown?

- Do you frequently get diverse opinions?

- Do you tackle problems others shy away from?

- Are you good at describing and presenting your ideas to others?

In an ideal world, one to three years from now, how would you like to answer these questions? What do you aspire to do differently?

If your answers in one to three years are different from today, how would you bridge that gap? Just one idea is enough to get started. What one thing will you begin doing?

LEVEL UP ACTIVITY FROM CHAPTER 12

Steps for Increasing Your Magnetism

- Assess where you are now. This can be as simple as recording your thoughts or your words. Make a list of how many are positive and how many aren't.

- Then describe what happens when you need something, like achieving a goal, and how you find the people who help you.

- Now, visualize three specific areas you want to be more magnetic (personal or professional).

- Write down two specific sentences you'll begin to speak out loud to others that would increase your magnetism. Maybe you choose something you often say that you'd like to change. The two specific sentences are what you will say in its place.

LEVEL UP ACTIVITY FROM CHAPTER 15

- Where could you spend some time? Is it in reflection or shedding some bricks you already are tired of carrying?

- If you're stuck on the deliberate steps of intention, find someone you know, like, and trust to help you through the process.

ABOUT THE AUTHOR

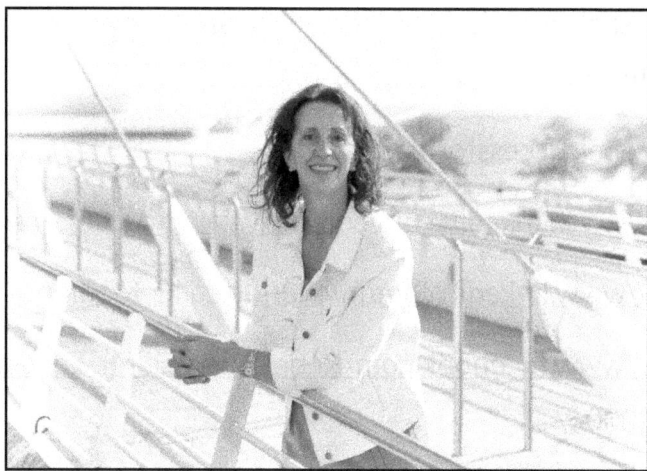

Charlotte's mission at Rebel Success for Leaders is to bring out the unconventional solutions genius in every team and every company she works with so that they can find a level of success they've never seen before.

Imagine you're winning in the market, you're attracting and keeping the best people, and you're innovating with unique and differentiated products and services. Charlotte is passionate about helping you become a magnet for extraordinary people, become the ideal destination organization, and learn to lead, grow, and sell fearlessly.

Charlotte has a PhD and over 20 years of experience, including her leadership at Kraft working with iconic brands including the launch of refrigerated meal kits, a redesign of Kraft Mac and Cheese, and packaging solutions for Oreo, Maxwell House, and Triscuit.

Today, she's a nationally recognized speaker and sought-after leadership consultant.

www.rebelsuccessforleaders.com

https://www.linkedin.com/company/rebel-success-for-leaders

https://www.linkedin.com/in/charlotteallenfoodinnovator/

https://www.facebook.com/Rebel-Success-for-Leaders-1029
31237920306/

REVIEWS

"Charlotte Allen is the visionary authority on leadership success. Her background as a top leader at Kraft for more than a decade, make her the go-to for the Fortune 500!"

—Sarah Victory, international award-winning
speaker and author of two best sellers
TheVictoryCompany.com

"Are you feeling limited by what you think you can achieve? With this book, *Rebel Success for Leaders*, you will be motivated to discover what you are truly capable of. You and your team will achieve much more than you ever thought possible! If you are ready to take yourself and your team to the next level, you have the specific tools in this powerful book to align, activate, and cultivate success. *Rebel Success for Leaders* highlights areas where you can identify real-life next steps to get the results you want and the results you need—quickly and effectively!"

—Wendy K. Benson, MBA, OTR/L and Elizabeth A. Myers, RN
Co-authors, *The Confident Patient*
2x2 Health: Private Health Concierge,
http://www.2x2health.com/

"In *Rebel Success for Leaders*, Charlotte Allen provides a clear framework for finding success by embracing your rebellious nature and why doing so will make you a better leader. Beyond igniting your own rebel success, **Charlotte's book outlines how you can spread this mindset to your team and positively impact your work environment.** The powerful, personal anecdotes from work and homelife that Charlotte weaves into her book make this both a page-turner and relatable read. Key topics like the qualities of a rebel leader, developing new teams, and avoiding burnout will resonate with new and seasoned leaders alike."

—Franny Gilman, Director of R&D, TerraMax

"*Rebel Success* has useful insights that will help you level up your leadership! Charlotte Allen is a storyteller at heart. That shows throughout *Rebel Success*, giving additional depth and perspective to the content. I appreciated the helpful callouts of actions I can take today. **Anyone looking to bring out their inner rebel and lean into leadership will benefit from the strategies in this book.**"

—Mark Steel, keynote speaker and sales consultant, founder of Peak Potential, and author of *Invincible Success: Sell with Confidence, Lead with Purpose, and Speak with Impact*

"Finally, a simple and easy-to-understand guide on Leadership Development. Leadership is not constrained to CEOs of a company. In fact, the leadership skills explained in this book, and the suggested exercises can be applied to deepen personal development, run a smoother household, foster community connections, and maximize results as a team player in the workplace. Charlotte encourages the reader to reflect upon their strengths and needs for further development, within the leadership attributes of creativity, influence, curiosity, and resilience."

—DR. KIMBERLY SCHEHRER, TEEN BREAKTHROUGH EXPERT, FOUNDER OF ACADEMY FOR INDEPENDENCE, AND PODCAST HOST OF "RAISING UNSTOPPABLE TEENS" ON VOICE AMERICA AND ITUNES

HTTPS://AFI4ME.COM/

"Rebel Success for Leaders is a very timely book with a wonderful blend of inspiring stories and actionable steps to take and create rebel leadership and culture within yourself or your organizations.** I found it a powerful change of pace to today's groupthink, which seems more prevalent within companies as society and media become more channeled in their messages. Charlotte Allen's personal stories are relevant today with Thelma calling her out to be more of a rebel thinker to Bill as a tough guy connecting to her rebel challenges about what is possible. Since I have had the pleasure of working with Charlotte, I learned a lot more about why she is such an effective rebel leader, as I have seen how in action many times."

—ROGER ZELLNER, PRESIDENT AND OWNER, ROGUE
ZEBRA CONSULTING, WWW.ROGUEZEBRA.COM

"To all serial 'disruptive innovators,' put this book on the top of your reading list! Where internal cultural challenges are often greater than those from external customers, tools to align, activate, and cultivate teams, as well as influence leadership, are critical to innovation success."

—LESLIE MACLIN, PRINCIPAL, ISTHMUS INNOVATION

"In her book, *Rebel Success for Leaders*, Charlotte Allen embarks on a journey of self-discovery with inspiring results. **Charlotte shares wonderful personal experiences teaching professionals how to lead, grow, and become fearless in the pursuit of success.**"

—Dr. Ivan Salaberrios, CEO, AIM Technical Consultants, Inc., HTTPS://AIMTECHNICAL.COM

"What I love so much about this book is considering the impact inside a company if everyone had enough inner rebel to make certain they were heard, and the leadership had enough inner rebel to listen. The solutions that can be uncovered give me chills; it's so cool! **I found this book to be smart, insightful, and disruptive versus the everyday leadership book!**"

—Kristin Crockett, CEO, Courageous Destiny, WWW.COURAGEOUSDESTINY.COM

"**If you want to accelerate from slow evolution to the super expressway of rapid innovation, Charlotte Allen's book is the key.** Elegantly written and filled with compelling stories, Ms. Allen gives readers everything they need to hire, sell, and above all, expand their organizations. Stop waiting for innovation. **You must read this book!**"

—Dr. Vince Racioppo, international speaker, author, and consultant; president of the Center for Expert Performance, Inc.

"Charlotte Allen has a gift for storytelling. Both as a professional speaker and an author, Charlotte paints a picture with her words. Whether listening to her or reading her book, I could identify with humbling and dramatic situations. *Rebel Success* **is the inescapable battle cry for you to step into your own Rebel Success.**"

—SUZANNE K. NANCE, WORLD RECORD HOLDER, SPEAKER, AND AUTHOR

HTTPS://WWW.LEADFROMTHETOP.COM/

www.ingramcontent.com/pod-product-compliance
Lightning Source LLC
Chambersburg PA
CBHW071607210326
41597CB00019B/3444